LEADERSHIP MATTERS

Leadership Matters

CONFRONTING THE HARD CHOICES FACING HIGHER EDUCATION

- - - - - - - - -

W. Joseph King & Brian C. Mitchell

JOHNS HOPKINS UNIVERSITY PRESS | *Baltimore*

Johns Hopkins University Press
2715 North Charles Street
Baltimore, Maryland 21218-4363
www.press.jhu.edu

Library of Congress Cataloging-in-Publication Data

Names: King, W. Joseph author. | Mitchell, Brian Christopher, 1953– author.
Title: Leadership matters : confronting the hard choices facing higher education /
    W. Joseph King and Brian C. Mitchell.
Description: Baltimore, Maryland : Johns Hopkins University Press, 2021. | Includes
    bibliographical references and index.
Identifiers: LCCN 2020057359 | ISBN 9781421442440 (hardcover) | ISBN 9781421442457
    (ebook)
Subjects: LCSH: Education, Higher—Aims and objectives—United States. | Universities
    and colleges—United States—Administration.
Classification: LCC LA227.4 .K49 2021 | DDC 378.73—dc23
LC record available at https://lccn.loc.gov/2020057359

A catalog record for this book is available from the British Library.

*Special discounts are available for bulk purchases of this book. For more information, please
contact Special Sales at specialsales@jh.edu.*

CONTENTS

We are living through an extraordinary moment in American higher education.

In our first book together, we spoke of three inflection periods. The first was after the Civil War, when 750,000 men and women died, which, among other developments, simultaneously caused a wave of private college mergers and the passage of the Morrill Land-Grant Act to jumpstart public higher education.[1] Such changes effectively reshaped the role of colleges in preparing an educated workforce for a more complex, industrializing economy.[2] The period also introduced new types of graduate and professional training at universities such as Johns Hopkins, the Massachusetts Institute of Technology, Caltech, and the University of Chicago.[3] The second period spanned the years from the Great Depression through World War II, culminating in the passage of the GI Bill, which positioned higher education as a ticket into the middle class. In that book, we argued that we have entered the third period of inflection, as colleges adapt to changing economic, social, cultural, technical, and demographic shifts now fully under way.[4] In every case, the common denominator is the rapidly changing circumstances leading to fundamental realignments, to which colleges and universities will have to adapt.

Similarly, what we could not anticipate while writing this book was the existential crisis created by the COVID-19 pandemic and a national reckoning with race in 2020. In President-elect Joe Biden's acceptance address on November 7, 2020, he argued that Americans must confront the devastating impact of COVID-19, restore economic prosperity to give Americans a "fair shot," improve their healthcare options, address systemic racism, and deal with escalating climate change. Each crisis that now President Biden identified cries out for some measure of leadership in higher education that extends across traditional classes of policy makers and thought partners. The searing image of George Floyd's death and the righteous anger over Breonna Taylor's murder provide incontrovertible evidence of the task ahead. The hard truth is that higher education leaders must use their intellectual capital to engage in the national discussions, thereby reclaiming a role they once played. Despite dramatic changes that profoundly affect the ability of colleges and universities to adapt, these institutions remain the repositories of American culture, the training ground for an educated citizenry, and America's intellectual and policy centers. Devoid of politics and self-interest, higher education leadership must quickly find a better way to make its voice heard.

Even before the coronavirus and the protests that have spread across the country, however, the telltale signs of a deepening higher education crisis were clear. America's colleges and universities operated with a failing tuition-based enrollment model, driven increasingly by rising financial aid discount rates, consumer unease over sticker prices, and the emergence of alternative degree and certificate-granting options. Many of them also suffered under a creaking, inertia-driven higher education bureaucracy, woefully inadequate state and federal financial partnerships, and an antiquated shared governance model of untutored volunteer trustees, faculty, and administrators.[5] It was clear even before the pandemic that future tuition increases will no longer support the academic enterprise. But colleges are also incubators for the workforce and economic engines that drive regional and the national economies.[6] As the American economy rebuilds, American higher education must reinsert itself more clearly into the national dialogue on what constitutes the public good.

That said, we passionately believe that America's colleges and universities are highly adaptable and the foundation that will best support a rebound in the American economy. Those that are truest to their mission, have a clear understanding of their role, and work to create efficiencies and economies of scale will adapt best. To do so they must form strategic partnerships and demonstrate flexibility and programmatic creativity. This book is a clarion call for leadership among the key stakeholders in higher education. The absence of confident, determined, and creative leadership will change the meaning, function, and outcome of the decentralized system of American higher education. It will affect America's ability to compete globally, will deter innovation, and will damage local, regional, and national economies.

Crises like these provide a unique opportunity to address the fundamental chasms that separate and divide Americans from one another. As the new economy emerges, the most telling question facing American higher education may be whether America's colleges and universities can successfully adapt to it. Initial decisions involved whether to pay back spring 2020 room and board, following immediately on how to assess the costs and impact of converting to online programming to replace, at least temporarily, brick-and-mortar pedagogy. Simultaneously, senior administrators needed to plan out the scale of their losses from summer, graduate, professional, and continuing education programs. It was almost impossible to project future revenue with certainty, based on an unprecedented softness in head counts, both for new and returning students.[7] The darkening deep recession clouds further exacerbated the uncertainty as more than 45.7 million Americans filed for unemployment by mid-June 2020. It was impossible to build and rely on a concrete budget based on the rapid economic collapse, with no promise of a return to prerecession employment levels. Joining Americans' growing uncertainty over their willingness to pay for higher education was the even larger problem of their capacity to do so. Across America there is an increasing sense that rudderless political leadership is causing confusion concerning what the economy might look like as it is being rebuilt.

The need to supplement income, bolster unemployment payments, and support businesses, large and small, emerged as first priorities, creating massive new deficits with little discussion on how to pay for them.[8] State and local governments, bulwarks of student aid, public university institutional support, and community college financing ran massive shortfalls, which will likely be structural over the longer term. The higher education community requested $50 billion in immediate support, for example, but received only $14 billion as part of the $3-trillion stimulus package to the economy.[9] Beyond budgeting, the open, pressing question by the early summer of 2020 was whether many American colleges and universities would open to accept traditional, residence-based classes in the fall. If they didn't, how long could they sustain a tuition-driven model without students?[10]

College and university leadership matters most precisely under such rapidly changing circumstances. Traditional ways of choosing leaders among key stakeholders may no longer fit the new paradigm. The financial tsunami facing American families may cause many students to reassess their commitment to the need for a traditional semester-based, four-year college degree. They may demand a different price point, or they may see advantages to certificate-based programming, three-year degrees, online programming on demand, or numerous other innovative, technology-grounded approaches, suited to the needs of the post-coronavirus workforce. The dismal demographics emerging will further contribute to the pressure on colleges and universities to adapt to a global work environment, where the crystal ball that can predict best how to proceed is murky. The older styles of leadership and the rules that govern it no longer necessarily apply.

It is a question of how to proceed under the new rules of engagement. Although every campus is different and shared governance can play out in numerous ways, leadership remains critical, especially when there are few historical lessons from previous generations of leaders to inform us in unprecedented times. America cannot exist in splendid isolation as the global economy recovers. Yet higher education must be the foundation upon which the "new normal," which fosters an educated workforce, is built. Its institutions must find the right fit in their leaders, discover how best to exercise and share leadership among stakeholder classes, and learn how to adapt quickly to a world that changed almost overnight. Every crisis carries with it challenges and opportunities, and the solution will play out differently on each campus. The question that must be answered is whether American colleges and universities can find the right mix of leadership, persistence, focus, and luck to prosper.

There are so many people to thank for their efforts to inspire, train, improve our understanding, and support us over the course of our writing. We suspect that many of them do not know the full impact that their mentorship and friendship has had upon us. They demonstrated by their words and deeds how best to lead a college. We mean to recognize and honor their contributions. Both individually and collectively, they shaped the character of the American college presidency, board stewardship, and faculty leadership. Each approached their responsibilities idiosyncratically and with different definitions of success. At critical moments, they made the difficult decisions that moved their institutions ahead, at times despite strong headwinds. We are grateful to them for their insight, perspective, and common sense.

We begin by extending our deep gratitude and thanks to Meridith Beck Mink, who assisted us with the research and development of the book. In her research for us, Meridith had the eye of a well-trained historian. Curious, thoughtful, methodical, and informed, she synthesized her findings with a crisp, unbiased analysis, which influenced our direction on a topic. Meridith was thorough and nonjudgmental, all the while encouraging us to think imaginatively about what to study, where to find available material, and how to present our findings and conclusions accurately. Our weekly Wednesday meetings were fruitful and fun. This book is a stronger effort because of Meridith's exemplary work.

It is impossible to recognize every college president who taught us about the job. This list is not fully inclusive, but it represents our best efforts. Many of the most experienced presidents have moved to other positions. Most remain close friends in their retirement. For simplicity, we have included the affiliation they held when we worked most closely with them or relied on them for advice. Arthur J. Rothkopf, Lafayette College, stands out for his encouragement and wisdom, which we continue to rely on. Also important to growth as higher education administrators were William (Bro) Adams, Colby College; Edward Ayers, University of Richmond; Larry Bacow, Harvard University; Esther Barazzone, Chatham University; William (Tom) Bogart, Maryville College; JoAnne Boyle, Seton Hill College (deceased); Christopher Breiseth, Wilkes University; Robert Bruce, Widener University; Jared Cohon, Carnegie Mellon University; Katie Conboy, Saint Mary's College; Thomas Courtice, Ohio Wesleyan University; Richard Creehan, Alderson Broaddus University; Michael Crow, Arizona State University; Jeffrey Docking, Adrian College; Rev. Edmund Dobbin, Villanova University; Jim Douthat, Lycoming College; and Richard Dunsworth, University of the Ozarks.

Other models of responsible presidential behavior include A. Lee Fritschler, Dickinson College; John Fry, Drexel University; Malcolm Gillis, Rice University (deceased); John Griffith, Presbyterian College; Bryon Grigsby, Moravian College; Mark Gearan, Hobart and William Smith Colleges; Christopher Hopey, Merrimack College; Tom Kepple, Juniata College; Neil Kerwin, American University; Tom Kessinger, Haverford College (deceased); and A. Richard Kneedler, Franklin & Marshall College. This list also includes Rev. Jim Lackenmier, King's College; Bette Landman, Arcadia University; Peter Likins, Lehigh University; Ted Long, Elizabethtown College; Roger Martin, Moravian College; Charlie McCormick, Schreiner University; and Mary Patterson McPherson, Bryn Mawr College. We also learned so much from Frederik Ohles, Nebraska Wesleyan University; Sr. Francesca Onley, Holy Family University; Rev. Joseph Allan Panuska, University of Scranton (deceased); Lynn Pasquerella, Mount Holyoke College; Rev. Nicholas Rashford, Saint Joseph's University; Jake Schrum, Emory & Henry College; Morton Schapiro, Northwestern University; Roy Shilling, Southwestern University; Daniel Sullivan, Allegheny College; Joel Thierstein, West Virginia Wesleyan College; Tim Thyreen, Waynesburg University; and Sr. Carol Jean Vale, Chestnut Hill College.

We also want to acknowledge our gratitude to the extraordinary colleagues, who served their higher education institutions and organizations in various capacities, with whom we have worked throughout our professional careers and have come to admire deeply. It's hard to narrow the list, but it includes George Boggs, American Association of Community Colleges; Alice Brown, Appalachian College Association; Mary DeCredico, Bucknell University; Richard Ekman, Council of Independent Colleges; Doug Foard, Phi Beta Kappa Association (deceased); Jon Hardesty, Collin County Community College; Charles Henry, Council on Library and Information Resources; Michael Keller, Stanford University; Carol Long, Willamette University; Philip Lewis and Eugene Tobin, Andrew W. Mellon Foundation; Ed Steinmetz, University of Scranton; James Walzel, Southwestern University; and David Warren, National Association of Independent Colleges and Universities. Arlene Peck, AICUP; Donna Falvo and Valerie Strimel, Washington & Jefferson College; Clarinda Foote, Lyon College; and Kelly Hottenstein, Melissa Schnars, and Marilyn Vargo were kind and patient tutors in our daily interactions.

Richard Gaumer, Academic Innovators, has been an especially valued colleague throughout this process.

Finally, we want to acknowledge with thanks the Council on Library and Information Resources, which provided the financial support to make this book possible. We are also grateful to our faculty and staff colleagues at Bucknell University, Emory & Henry College, George Mason University, Merrimack College, Rice University, Texas Christian University, the University of Massachusetts at Lowell, the University of Rochester, the University of Washington, and Washington & Jefferson College. Thanks also to colleagues at the Annapolis Group, the Association of Independent Colleges and Universities of Pennsylvania, Connexions, the National Association of Independent Colleges and Universities State Executives, the National Merit Scholarship Corporation, the National Institute for Technology in Liberal Education, the Pennsylvania Selection Committee for the Rhodes Scholarship, the Patriot League, the President's Athletic Conference, and our professional and institutional accreditors. We also want to thank faculty colleagues in one particular group: newly tenured and early-stage faculty, who consistently demonstrated their enthusiasm, dedication, and strong work ethic in our professional relationships with them. They showed how dynamic and creative faculties can be on a college campus.

This is our second book together. We remain colleagues and friends—no small feat by itself, but a happy and productive experience.

LEADERSHIP MATTERS

Introduction

American colleges and universities have never been particularly stable or sustainable enterprises, as measured by their financial performance. Most rely upon philanthropy or government support to balance their budgets. If they have an endowment, it is usually modest compared to the institution's operating costs. Many of their assets are in buildings and equipment, which require constant maintenance, updating, and replacement. Therefore, these institutions are especially susceptible to financial downturns. This is not a new state in American higher education but, rather, a perpetual one.

The author's (King) institution, Lyon College, was founded as Arkansas College in 1872, the year before the start of the Long Depression of the 1870s. In a history of the college, Brooks Blevins writes, "By any standard, Arkansas College was a poor college . . . Even when compared to the typical western college, Arkansas College received a weak financial sendoff. The process of college founding took place so rapidly in a depressed era and state and Batesville was such an out-of-the-way place, that insufficient funds plagued the school immediately."[1] Arguably, the college did not experience real financial success until the 1950s. This postwar era, with its demographic and financial expansion, was a boon for higher education in general.

The Great Recession and its aftermath are having a predictable negative effect on higher education. The diminished wealth of the middle class, in particular, is causing serious financial stress for colleges and universities. Nelson Schwartz writes, "The scars of the financial crisis and the ensuing Great Recession are still with us, just below the surface. The most profound of these is that the uneven nature of the recovery compounded a long-term imbalance in the accumulation of wealth."[2] Median household income has been stagnant for almost twenty years, while wealth for these families has contracted.[3] Schwartz further notes, "When the bubble burst, the bedrock investment for many families was wiped out by a combination of falling home values and too much debt. A decade after this debacle, the typical middle-class family's net worth is still more than $40,000 below where it was in 2007, according to the Federal Reserve."[4] For most families, a college education is their second-largest investment, after their home.[5] With the decline in their financial resources, these families struggle mightily to cover college costs. This situation is unlikely to improve in the coming decades of ever-increasing wealth disparity.

Harvard University, the country's oldest and best resourced institution, noted in its 2017 financial report:

> This year's operating surplus . . . may represent a high-water mark for the foreseeable future, however, due to the broad and ongoing revenue pressures in higher education . . . Since the 1950's, higher education in the United States has been a growth industry, and has enjoyed demographic increases in student populations, generally steady economic expansion, increases in federal research funding, and robust investment markets. This picture has changed. Higher education has matured as an industry and revenues are under pressure as student numbers have plateaued, tuition costs reach limits of affordability, federal research support is threatened, and expectations for returns in the investment markets are muted. The industry is showing financial strain, even in

these comparatively healthy economic times, with the recent closures, shrinkages, and mergers of smaller, less well-positioned schools."[6]

This is a remarkable analysis for many reasons, not the least of which is that it was made in the annual report of one of the world's most successful institutions of higher learning. It speaks to the precarity of colleges and universities when students and families experience long-term financial hardship.

This hardship can present itself in other ways. The most dramatic is demographic. In 2018, the birthrate in the United States hit a thirty-two-year low. The fertility rate was the lowest ever recorded by the federal government. In fact, births have fallen during ten of the past eleven years.[7] This change in demographics will play out dramatically over the coming decades. High school graduation rates are forecasted to fall substantially in the Northeast, the Ohio Valley, and the Midwest.[8] Many of these graduates will not go on to college, and thus the number of college-going students will contract in most regions, with the exception of Texas and the Mountain West. Unfortunately, many of the regions predicted to see the greatest contractions also have the largest numbers of colleges and universities. This will inevitably lead to even more strain on these institutions as they experience declines in their primary market.

Another trend playing out simultaneously is the increasing numbers of lower-income college students. "Low-income students now enroll in college at a higher rate than their middle-income peers," observes Preston Cooper.[9] He goes on to note that "in 1986, 73% of top-quintile high school graduates went on to college, compared to 37% of bottom-quintile graduates. That made for an 'enrollment gap' between rich and poor students of 36 percentage points. But as of 2016, the gap has narrowed to just 16 percentage points." This is terrific news from the standpoint of equality. However, for institutions struggling to balance their budgets, it is yet another challenge. In its 2018 survey, *Inside Higher Ed* found that more than 80 percent of admissions directors, at both public and private institutions, were moderately or very concerned about filling classes.[10] This sort of existential dread is now com-

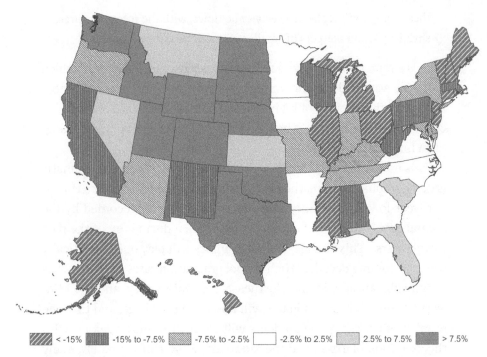

| /// < -15% | ‖‖‖ -15% to -7.5% | \\\ -7.5% to -2.5% | ☐ -2.5% to 2.5% | ▨ 2.5% to 7.5% | ■ > 7.5% |

Figure I.1 Forecasted growth in high school graduates, 2012–2032. *Source:* Nathan D. Grawe, *Demographics and the Demand for Higher Education* (Baltimore: Johns Hopkins University Press, 2018), 16.

mon, and it calls upon college leaders to be "keepers of the faith" in a way that has not been required for generations. It also calls upon them to be strategic visionaries in embracing change that is equal to the task of confronting these great challenges.

This is not an argument for some sort of unitary executive or brash entrepreneur. Quite the opposite; it is an argument for college leaders who understand and appreciate shared governance. A president is part of shared governance but does not dominate the "sharing"; rather, there are coequal branches of institutional governance. A good president understands the reach and limitations of the job. She or he should also be a fulcrum for the trustees and faculty, challenging them to take up fully their responsibility as shared governors. Shared governance does not work without trustees who zealously embrace their governance and fiduciary roles. Likewise, shared governance does not

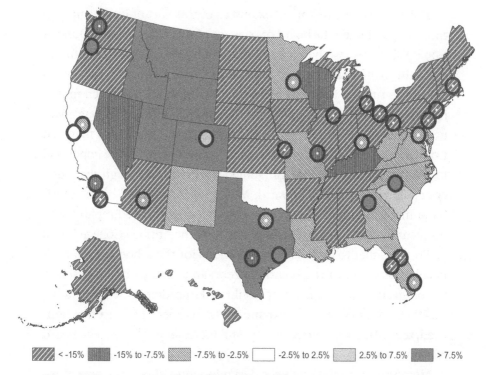

Figure I.2 Forecasted growth in college-going students, 2012–2029. *Source:* Grawe, *Demographics and the Demand for Higher Education*, 49.

work without faculty who show the same zeal with regard to the curriculum and academic programs. Strategic change cannot be accomplished without both groups working together in common cause.

This likely requires broad retraining, a different system of presidential selection, a deeper effort to build a bench of potential candidates, and increased specialization (e.g., presidents who understand academics and the world beyond the college gates). Presidents fail because they do not understand the job, are unable to adjust to it, or are unwilling to remake themselves based on what the job needs rather than what they want or expect from it. This applies equally to board chairs and provosts. All three leaders must serve in the spirit of always doing what is right for the institution. This service is often selfless, requiring long hours and a commitment to fully embody the institution, from sweatshirt to kilt.

There are strong historical examples of this sort of leadership. Arthur Morgan joined the board of trustees of Antioch College in June of 1919.[11] With only two hundred fifty students, the college was in financial ruin. It had an outdated curriculum, and students struggled to afford the tuition. Founded by Horace Mann in 1853, Antioch might, in Mann's eyes, become "the little Harvard of the West." It was coeducational and integrated from its founding, with a faculty of men and women devoted to these egalitarian ideas.[12] However, these hopes had long faded by the time Morgan joined the board. Although the trustees could not see a way forward, Morgan was intrigued by the moribund institution. Aaron Purcell writes, "Morgan moved rapidly with his planning for Antioch. On August 3, 1919, the Antioch College Board of Trustees met to discuss new directions for the school. Morgan officially presented to the board his reorganization plans. In essence, the program of work and study would make academic life more holistic."[13] He laid out goals of expanding the student body to five hundred, recruiting top-notch faculty, and increasing salaries. The board was interested.

Morgan was a civil engineer designing a flood control system for the Miami (Ohio) River Valley, and so he demurred when the Antioch board asked him to consider the presidency in early 1920. Purcell writes, "Morgan's claim that he originally had no interest in becoming president was genuine, largely because he knew that academic credentials were a prerequisite for higher education administration and he possessed none. But by the spring of 1920, unable to attract potential presidential candidates and in the spirit of his practical education mantra, Morgan reconsidered his ascension to the post."[14] Morgan moved quickly to recruit new trustees to the small, Ohio-centric board. Ellery Sedgwick, editor of *Atlantic Monthly*, Charles Kettering, vice president of General Motors, and Edwin Gray, former dean of the Harvard Business School, agreed to join the board. Within a year, seven of twenty trustees were from outside Ohio.[15] In that same year, the Antioch Plan was conceived. Robert Barde summarizes, "The Antioch Plan encompassed both practical work and cultural studies. The small student body was divided into two groups. Half worked for five weeks while the remainder studied at college. At the end of the period, the two groups exchanged positions."[16] This structure allowed students to earn enough money to pay tuition and support themselves, while still completing a degree within six years.[17]

Before Morgan began, Antioch had only thirteen full-time employees, and only two held a PhD degree. Just like the trustees, he moved quickly to remedy the situation. Through aggressive national searches, twenty-five teaching faculty and two librarians were added in 1921. Morgan even tried to recruit John Dewey to the faculty. Failing that, many nationally known scholars did join the faculty.[18] The school thrived, even during the hardest years of the Great Depression, due primarily to the innovative cooperative work plan. Morgan was recruited by Franklin D. Roosevelt to be the founding chairman of the Tennessee Valley Authority. "When he left for the T.V.A. in 1933, the student body had increased to 560 and had some 150 cooperating employers around the country," notes his *New York Times* obituary.[19]

In 1958, Texas A&M College was a rural, land-grant college with just over seven thousand students. Aggie alumnus Durwood B. Varner, vice president of Michigan State University and future chancellor of the University of Nebraska, laid out its deficiencies: mandatory military training, hazing, all-male student body, low faculty morale, alumni dedicated to tradition over change.[20] That year James Earl Rudder, also an alumnus and a war hero, was named vice president and shortly thereafter president (Hatfield, 304, 313). Like Varner and the board, he could see that things would have to change to modernize the college. Nevertheless, he was measured and careful in his approach. His top priority was to hire a chief academic officer with the academic credentials and experience he lacked. Wayne C. Hall, an eminent plant scientist, was named dean of the graduate school (317). Hatfield writes about his interview, "Hall described A&M as a sleeping giant with unlimited potential that lacked only leadership and vision" (318). This aligned with Rudder's emerging vision to develop Texas A&M into a graduate and research institution, a full-fledged university (319).

The transformation would be methodical. Rudder established two study groups, one internal and one external, each including representatives from many constituencies. Hatfield explains, "Each group would examine Texas A&M for a year before recommending goals on how A&M should change to achieve preeminence by 1976, the hundredth anniversary of its founding" (Hatfield, 324). The first group, known as the Committee on Aspirations, was chaired by Hall and included twenty-four faculty, staff, and students. Rudder provided the charge: "Look at A&M College with the future in mind, visualizing how all of us as a team can improve this institution and better serve the people of Texas, especially the youth of this state (325). The second group, known as the Century Council, comprised one hundred leading citizens of Texas, of which fifty-six were alumni, selected by the board. Its charge was more general; Rudder told its members that "the future of Texas in large measure depends on how successfully its institutions of higher education plan now to meet the challenges anticipated in the next fifteen years (325).

The Century Council's resulting recommendations were broadly aspirational: "The attainment of excellence should be the long-range aim of all activities of the College" (Hatfield, 326). However, there were some breakthroughs, such as a recommendation for "careful and objective studies" of coeducation (328). Hall's internal committee, on the other hand, made strong specific recommendations: construction of a new library, a revised faculty tenure policy, increases in salary levels, recognition for outstanding teaching and research, ending compulsory military training, etc. (327). Rudder and Hall took up this agenda, as well as a broader societal agenda to admit women and African Americans. Rudder used his considerable political clout to enlist Lyndon B. Johnson's aid in these last two efforts. In 1965, Texas A&M University (renamed two years earlier) was coeducational and integrated, and military training was optional for the first time in its history (329). Hatfield concludes, "Texas A&M's self-evaluations in 1962, consolidated as the Blueprint for Progress, spawned four initiatives that by 1966 had laid the foundation for the institution that A&M would become over the next half-century" (329).

These two examples also show the need for college and university presidents—individually and collectively—to reassert their role as thought leaders on matters that affect American society. In doing so, they should steer clear of the politics but focus on the dimensions of social good, economic inequality, and the power of intellectual thought. They should also emerge as business leaders, reshaping the role of American colleges and universities as critical business enterprises, locally, regionally, nationally, and internationally. The engines of innovation are stoked by these institutions and their graduates; therefore, the presidents should not shy away from a leadership role that reflects this reality.

One thing is for certain: strategic change will be necessary for almost every institution, even the strongest, in the coming decades. Harvard's 2017 financial report concludes:

> In the years ahead, however, it will be increasingly difficult to balance budgets in a new era of constrained revenue growth, and also, inevitably, when the current economic expansion wanes. We raise this not as a matter of discouragement, but simply to signal to the University's many friends, supporters, alumni, faculty, students, and staff that the University, and its Schools and units, will need to further adjust to the environment, change, and embrace new ways of extending Harvard's excellence in the future."[21]

True excellence should be the goal of every academic institution and its leaders. These institutions are currently facing financial and demographic challenges to their excellence greater than any since the Great Depression. At this critical time, their success will depend on leaders who can harness the strengths of the institution and its governing constituencies. It has been generations since such leaders were needed, so in a substantial sense, they will have to be made—born of adversity.

1

Presidents, Provosts, and Board Chairs

American colleges and universities operate under a system of governance shared among three groups: trustees, faculty, and the administration. This system is fundamentally distinct from that of the corporate world, and it shapes how colleges operate, who makes the decisions, and what timelines guide their actions. The work of these three leaders is truly "make-or-break" for the institution. This is even truer in times of distress and change. On almost any college campus, process is king. The outcome of that process may be anticlimactic, but what's often more important is how the three groups reach a decision. Although the circumstances vary across campuses, there is an implied code of conduct that shapes how each governing group relates to the others. This relationship also affects how other key stakeholder groups, including students, alumni, parents, and donors, fit into the decision-making process that determines the priorities that shape an effective institutional strategy.

In this chapter, we look at the role of the three foremost leaders of a college or university: the president, the provost, and the board chair. Two of these leaders, the provost and the board chair, align with specific shared governance constituencies: the faculty and the trustees. The president serves as bridge between the two and may actually be a member of both bodies. Each drives the institution forward in different ways. We argue that there are three types of president: presider, change agent, and strategic visionary, and we discuss the merits and perils of each. Make no mistake about it—leadership is the dynamic upon which a higher education institution builds momentum. It works best when key leaders are prepared, understand their role, and work to make their fellow leaders successful. But therein lies the problem, because many leaders are unprepared. Others step up to a job that they are unqualified to perform, while some assume that they were born to the presidency. The worst of them—often board chairs and presidents—come with a preconceived agenda that fails to reflect how an institution works, except perhaps in their own mind. That is especially problematic when an institution is under stress. We also examine how each of the three leaders is selected and evaluated. Diligence and success in this process is a major driver of institutional success. Finally, we make recommendations about how these leadership roles and selection processes must evolve to continue to be relevant.

Some commentators have argued for the radical redesign of the shared governance system to make American colleges and universities more efficient and responsive to their stakeholders, claiming that shared governance has outlived its usefulness. They find that governance inhibits a nimble and agile response to crisis and opportunity. Detractors believe that shared governance props up the status quo. They see collegiate governance as the place where originality and creativity go to die, by creating so many layers of review, with timelines unsuited to a quick business decision. They ask, How can you run an institution if decisions go unmade during fall, holiday, and spring breaks, as well as throughout the summer? How can you run a twelve-month business on an eight-month schedule? Further, the detractors assert that shared governance introduces an unhealthy tension among governance groups reinforced by how each group perceives its role and each other.[1]

In fact, shared governance is the most defining feature of the way colleges operate. It has served American society well precisely because it fosters a deliberative, balanced understanding of what makes American colleges and universities unique.[2] Higher education creates and builds the intellectual capital that shapes how American society evolves as a democracy. Shared governance is an internal checks-and-balance system, which prevents any one stakeholder group from becoming the loudest voice in the room. It assumes civility and transparency. When something goes wrong in governance on a college campus, it is most likely that one of the three leadership groups has overstepped its authority.[3]Authoritarian presidents seldom succeed on a campus, although presidents must exercise whatever leadership they think is appropriate, based on the cards dealt to them when they take office.[4] The president, the head of academic leadership, and the board chair must each understand that his or her success is dependent on how well shared governance works. Each leader must make the other better, and failure to do so can stop an institution's momentum in its tracks. This is especially true in times of distress and change.

Presidents fall into three broad categories: the presider, the change agent, and the strategic visionary (table 1.1). The presider is usually hired to calm the waters following periods of rapid change or significant or unanticipated disruption. These presidents often come from the faculty, through the ranks of dean and provost, and may be selected internally from among these ranks. They are comforting to the campus community because they understand the daily workings of a college. These presidents have special talent in keeping an ear to the ground for issues of internal campus concern, and they often assume a kind of *pater familias* role. They approach the job as a cross between a ceremonial mayor and a super-provost. Many see themselves as the moral conscience of the community. People, programs, and facilities remain in place; indeed, it is possible through the combination of tuition increases, auxiliary revenue, and judicious use of debt for the campus to continue to evolve successfully. Presider presidents protect the present, uphold the status quo, and are often well-liked, particularly by internal campus constituencies.

The evolution of a college or university is somewhat cyclic. Presider

Table 1.1. The three types of college president

Presider	Change agent	Strategic visionary
• Status quo	• Challenges status quo	• Focuses on strategic plan
• Continuity and tradition	• Innovative	• Drives innovation
• Stability	• Impatient for change	• Continuous improvement
1890s, 1920s, 1950s, 1990s	1940s, 1960s, 1980s, 2000s	1870s, 1930s, 2010s, 2020s

presidents can serve a valuable purpose because, like faculty, they uphold tradition and protocol. They often take a limited, circumscribed interest in events beyond the college gates and play a limited role in government affairs at the state and federal levels. They see the college or university as an academic enterprise, sometimes to the detriment of the institution's increasing need to be an important economic engine for their region. Their thought leadership can be more cerebral than practical, offering valuable opinions, for example, on questions of diversity, campus safety, and the responsible use of alcohol among students. They are less inclined to speak to matters of national higher education policy and seldom have a close relationship with elected local, state, and federal officials. Campuses can sometimes seem like communities whose occupants live in a world that they wish existed. For presider presidents, it is critical to keep that world alive. They are often excellent collaborators and responsible strategic partners, but they seldom lead through creativity and initiative. Boards continue to select presider presidents, even though they reached their height of popularity as a logical choice at the end of the twentieth century.

Change-agent presidents are confident, decision-driven, and often impatient about results. They come with an agenda and are certain about what their tenure means for their campus. They are sometimes outgoing and work hard to develop a strategic plan. Many change-agent presidents openly reject certain traditions and protocol in favor of embodying change. They often run campuses that have very different needs from process-driven residential colleges. Search committees attract these presidents to campuses when challenges outweigh opportunities, and the feeling at hiring is that change is needed. Boards may be seeking answers to the challenges they face, the restoration of brand and reputation, or a desire to compete more directly with aspirant schools. There is a danger, however, when the board's intentions run counter to the commitment of the campus to change.

Change-agent presidents are often remarkable innovators, who put new combinations of people, programs, and facilities into place. They are typically creative, efficient, and a good reputational move for the institution. They may seek to increase net tuition revenue almost immediately. They are unfazed by criticism of too much change on the campus; indeed, the changes they propose often breathe new life into the institution in hindsight. Further, they are responsive to what the search committee said that it wanted. The problem is often the cognitive dissonance between what the search committee wanted and what the campus will tolerate. Change agents can be a blur of motion, often maintaining broad external contacts. Boards select change-agent presidents to reflect broader shifts in higher education, most recently demonstrating an uptick during the upheaval caused by the Great Recession, but presidents of this type can wear out their welcome quickly.

The final type of president is the strategic visionary. Like the change agent, these presidents ignore the status quo, but they understand that institutions need to ground their efforts in research, both internally and compared against their peers and aspirants. They drive innovation and work hard to form a consensus, with the goal of empowering the campus to reinvent its future. Among the three types described in figure 1, the strategic visionary develops a plan that is relentlessly strategic, looking first at the college's financial health to determine where opportunities lie. They link strategy, revenue, and expenses to move beyond a change agent, who may only see how challenges can be met through growing net tuition revenue or increasing the level of debt. They plan for an institution's future that may extend out decades, even though updated, targeted, and more time-defined additions to a strategic plan will likely be required. The strength of the strategic visionary is that she or he understands how to place the institution in the world rather than grow it internally and organically, like an isolated city upon a hill.

Boards most often choose presidents who act as strategic visionaries at a time of upheaval in American higher education, when challenges extend beyond those facing an individual campus. In our recent book, *How to Run a College: A Practical Guide for Trustees, Faculty, Administrators and Policymakers*, we argued that there have been three critical inflection points in the history of American higher education.[5] The first was in the 1870s, during the upheaval caused by the high death toll among men in the Civil War, together with a national recession that saw the merger of many private institutions, the growth of new ones as the frontier expanded westward, and the passage of key acts to create publicly supported institutions to train in fields such as agriculture and teaching, symbolized by the Morrill Land-Grant Act. The second occurred in the 1930s, sparked by the Great Depression. Many institutions suffered dramatically, contemplated mergers, and became training grounds for subsequent war efforts in the Second World War, opening a period of government-directed expansion with the Serviceman's Readjustment Act of 1944, better known as the G.I. Bill. We are now at the third inflection point, as American colleges and universities face the collapse of their pricing model, declining demographics, shifts in public perception, growing technological change, and near depression-levels of unemployment—all worsened by the pandemic.[6]

Each of these three points of inflection can be defined as a kind of extended emergency in higher education. They underscore the critical need for strategic-visionary presidents to craft long-term strategies, and they support a shift away from presider and change-agent presidents. The older operating models that supported colleges no longer work and have created a period of deteriorating fiscal health, with no clear plan beyond increasing financial aid or developing new programs to work through this uncertainty. Most colleges also suffer from weak strategy, driven by failures within shared governance, and are at best incremental in their approach to change on a college campus.[7] Moreover, ambiguity caused by forces that higher education cannot shape—in technology, demographics, changing consumer preferences, and workforce development—require a strategic view that incorporates and embraces inevitable uncertainty. This is the moment when presidential leadership, developed in consort with trustees and faculty, must kick in.

If our argument holds true, whether colleges and universities become winners or losers will not depend simply upon their weathering this third inflection point through marginal change, through delay, or by hiding in plain sight until the higher education world stabilizes. In a period of change and uncertainty, it will not simply be the institutions with the largest endowments that will emerge unscathed. Setting aside the type and purpose of each institution, those that fare best will be the colleges and universities that recognize opportunity during instability and upheaval. In quiet conversations across the country, there are deepening discussions about how to face the future.[8] Those that adapt and innovate will likely remain the most relevant to American society. While we are optimistic, there is a long and deepening crisis that sets the stage for presidents who are strategic visionaries. This raises the critical question of how good leadership translates into a solution-driven strategic agenda. Put in other terms, what does a president do?

The president serves as the keeper of the faith and defender of the realm, especially during turbulent times. While the faculty have the responsibility to provide continuity across presidential administrations, good presidents must first respect the history and tradition of their institution. It is important to embrace the traditions—from the college song to the school colors—and build on a history that demonstrates strength in leadership by protecting the continuity of tradition. A new president is an outsider, and some, especially alumni and alumni trustees, will see the president as an administrator rather than as their new campus community leader. The ability to embrace a campus community rather than dominate it is an important early skill to pull out of the presidential tool kit.[9]

Presidents are, after all, the most transient players in shared governance, with an average tenure of approximately seven years.[10] New presidents are offered jobs based on parameters that fit each institution, and there is no single skill set that determines a successful presidential tenure. Candidates should be wary of presidential profiles that seek superhuman skills, especially if the profile fails to offer an honest appraisal of what works and does not work on the campus.[11] What, then, is the first sign of effective leadership in a prospective president? It is likely the ability to match the description of the offer, should one be made, to an understanding of the reality they will face on that first day as the new campus leader. The offer and the reality often present very different perspectives, as many new presidents learn painfully later. This makes the role of the search committee and how the campus conducts the search enormously significant. Candidates with well-earned reputations, especially sitting presidents, put themselves at serious risk in an open, public search.[12] Presidential candidates rely heavily, therefore, on the liaison assigned from the executive search firm. Perhaps the most important quality in college leadership is the ability to listen. For a president, this begins with an open, back-and-forth communication with the search firm to test questions, concerns, and opportunities that candidates might see. A good search firm can determine for a presidential candidate whether the profile provided is accurate and if the campus community is committed to what it wrote.[13] One of the first keys to solid presidential leadership is to determine if the campus community understands itself and its role more broadly in higher education.

It is important, therefore, for the selection committee, the board, and the faculty to think carefully about their campus interactions after a presidential selection, to set the stage for the president's arrival. How the shared governance leadership presents the president, explains the reasons behind the choice, and builds campus support after the selection announcement will determine in part what climate will await the new president. If they are true to the selection committee criteria, the others who share governance need to brand the president effectively by indicating the kind of leadership the campus can expect to see. They must use the selection committee profile as a kind of primer to establish how the president will fit into the campus community, building enthusiasm and a sense of momentum that will carry over into the first months of a new president's tenure.[14]

If a presidential candidate is not clear-headed about the prospective job, then the attractiveness of the job will likely mask good judgment in other instances. The search speaks more generally to one of the fundamental tenets of presidential leadership: trust, but verify. There are occasions when there are no warning signs. There are times when the politics of the point in time may disguise the way things might play out after the job has been accepted. Changes mandated, often by an accrediting agency, may be accepted in principle but violated in practice by the board and on campus. They may be reinterpreted by trustees to reflect views that are at odds, for example, with the spirit and direction of the accreditor's requirements, or they may simply be ignored over time. While no one can predict the future, presidential candidates should consult broadly with the executive search firm, trusted colleagues, and widely across the new campus community to make the most informed decision possible.[15]

Once the job has been accepted, it is critical to remember two basic facts. First, as the new president, you carry the hopes and aspirations of a wide community of stakeholders. You must act as both the key campus leader and as a facilitator, embodying your community's vision, which may vary dramatically by stakeholder. Second, everyone within the campus gates works for you, but you also work for them. While presidents can maintain warm professional relationships with colleagues across all levels, they cannot turn these relationships into personal ones during their tenure.

The board chair is often the best person to explain how the president will engage with them. There will usually be a significant group of influential faculty, presumably drawn in part from the ranks of the search committee, who will contribute to the advance branding of a president. Presidents preside as the chief administrator over a business, but they are also equivalent to the mayor of a small city and often more a collaborator and facilitator than their corporate counterparts.[16] Most importantly, the president is the bridge between the trustees and the faculty and staff. A significant part of this work is coherently and consistently explaining one group to the other. It is important early on to review the mechanisms and venues that provide for structured interactions between trustees, faculty, and staff in order to normalize appropriate and regular conversation among the groups. Normalizing relationships and crafting common ground can help set the level of and rules on transparency among the groups, simultaneously opening and constraining the communications among them.

Presidents also have a role to play that extends beyond the campus. This takes a variety of forms. Presidents run an economic engine that generates jobs and revenue for the community. It is important to meet local, state, regional, and federal officials early into the job.[17] The long history of town-gown relations suggests that the local community often feels that neighborhood problems are not addressed sufficiently, typically extending well beyond questions of off-campus housing and student conduct. Presidents should keep in mind that a good strategic plan embraces the role of a college in its region. The region is the equivalent of the first impression made by the college on prospective applicants when they visit. A dynamic economy, with the college clearly in full partnership with the community, sends a powerful message to prospective applicants and other constituencies about how an institution sees its role in the world.[18] Even fundraising—an important part of the president's job—is about relationships, often nurtured best off campus.

One of the most time-consuming and rewarding parts of a president's job is the cultivation of major donors, which builds on the relationships established over a period longer than the tenure of a president. The expectations of the president, the fundraising team, and the potential donor must, therefore, be well understood by all parties. There must be a practical recognition among the team of fundraisers about what a president can reasonably be expected to do, with the expectations varying, depending upon the size of the school, the maturity of the advancement program, and the depth of the fundraising pool. Beyond trustees, presidents should be given a list with a set number of major donors, based upon good research, the history of affiliation with the institution, and the potential that exists, especially when working with new donors. Presidents must also understand that donors can be cultivated both for money and influence. And it is essential for the team to understand that the president cannot close every gift.

At some point, presidents will lead a capital campaign, most likely comprehensive in nature. It changes the president's work schedule, because the campaign shifts the emphasis and direction of the president's work from planning to execution. Fundraising is one way to meet part of the commitment created by the approval of a new strategic vision, the adoption of a financial plan, and the rollout of an effective communications program. A good capital campaign is only one tool that emerges from the financial plan that funds strategy. The presidents who are the best fundraisers understand that they are playing long ball, with most gifts deferred, delayed, or paid out over time, often beyond their own tenure. In many respects, large delayed gifts can ensure sustainable transformative change. But the more perceptive presidents will recognize that a broadening base of support and a growing annual fund are the best way to pay the bills.[19]

It is a mistake for a president to willfully create imbalance across the full range of presidential duties. Leaders require self-policing to allot limited time to the various duties that leadership demands. Further, the allocation of time spent across duties will change over time. In addition, much of the job of president requires attention to areas that a president does not enjoy or is not prepared to perform by leaning on previous job experience. The mix of senior staff must accommodate what a strategic vision demands through their combined individual skills, what talent the president may or may not possess, and what path the president's vision lays out for the future. A basic truth for senior leadership, particularly presidents, undergirds everything: Learn the job. Take time to grasp those parts of the job that you understand least.

Perhaps most importantly, presidents should develop a network of friends and mentors who have held the job before and who stand apart from internal relationships and those with the board chair.[20] Their counsel can be invaluable when new challenges arise. Implied in this argument is an intangible trait that separates and defines the leadership of the best presidents: empathy. Search committees should assess candidates to see if their ability to be empathetic matches the expectations anticipated in campus culture. Presidents may differ by personality. They may be introverts, extroverts, or some hybrid form of both. They may be consummate diplomats in their dealings with others, "in your face" leaders, or austere and detached, among many personality types. But they must always be empathetic. Key stakeholders can spot the absence of empathy immediately.[21] It weakens any leadership style and makes implementation of a strategic vision much more difficult. Presidents are presented with a thousand teachable moments, whether public or private. Perhaps better than any other, how presidents deal with personal tragedies in the campus community can define the character of their leadership. These will be the moments that presidents reflect back on after their years of service have been completed. Put in other terms, good presidents lead through their humanity, their ability to listen, their willingness to go the extra mile, and sometimes just by showing up. And above all they must be genuine.

The president's relationship across the campus community is defined in part by differences among the stakeholder classes. There must be, for example, a level of trust and confidence in the institution's chief financial officer. CFO's hold the financial keys to presidential vision. They are the enforcers of budget priorities that ration available revenue. They lay out the financial plan and determine how to pay for the tactics that shape the strategic vision. The relationship between the president and the CFO in large part determines the success and effectiveness of the senior team in presenting a unified funding message. But of all the relationships that inform and contextualize the ability of the president to lead, none is more important than the professional give-and-take that presidents have with the provost, or the designated senior academic leader. A college or university is fundamentally an academic enterprise. Its academic program defines it mission and sets in stone the principles and processes that govern it. Colleges are their own economies, but as we have argued, they are not widget factories.

The academic side, led by the provost, is where ideas are incubated and where cultural transmission is passed along to the generations that follow.

The position of provost reminds most presidents that there is a difference between the role of an institution as an academic enterprise and as an economic engine. The provost has the most difficult job on campus. A good provost understands the importance of the first role, but a great one thoughtfully executes with an eye to integrating and explaining to faculty the importance of both. Presidents seek qualities in a provost that they may not have or anticipate might be better found in a full-time academic leader. There is a difference in the two roles; indeed, selection as a provost is not an automatic prequel to a presidency. The best provosts have a unique skill set, which emerges from long years of distinguished service on the faculty. As a group, they are more homogenous than the applicant pool for presidents; they focus more heavily on programmatic initiative and people management than do other senior leaders.[22] This is why some institutions—Williams, for example—rotate their position of dean of the faculty. Most institutions require a tight series of prerequisites for the positions of provost and dean drawn from faculty service.

Interestingly, many provosts increasingly have no desire to become presidents.[23] Provosts serve the president, advocate for the faculty, and nurture and protect the academic program, supporting simultaneously tradition, process, innovation, and change. Provosts play a critical role in faculty leadership, managing the business of academics confidently, identifying senior faculty leadership, and nurturing junior faculty as they integrate into the academic culture. Provosts drive process but are not driven by it. The best of them constantly search for excellent teaching and research. They work with the president and CFO to fund creativity to ameliorate some of the worst aspects of campus cultural inertia. They also translate to the president, senior staff, board, and other key stakeholders both the tangible and intangible needs and concerns of the faculty. In doing so, they are often perceived as a kind of deputy president. At most institutions, the provost steps in for the president whenever the president is unavailable.

To build a successful partnership, presidents must forge an understanding with a provost whom they respect and admire, knowing that in their absence or in unanticipated crisis, the provost must have the leadership skills, gravitas, and moral authority to step into the president's job. The most experienced provosts assume a wide range of duties. Recently, many institutions have combined academic and student affairs, with the many departments, centers, institutes, and libraries associated with them.[24] Effectively, the provost administers a large portion of the budget and a good deal of the discretionary money available. Presidents should always be mindful to keep a tight rein on an institution's budget, but not hamstring the ability of the provost to nurture and reward faculty, staff, and student innovation.

Given the changing nature of the modern presidency, it is critical that provosts also "play up" to a role that is also being redefined. Provosts must understand athletics, especially as tensions increase between athletics and academics.[25] They must interpret key business terms and work with the faculty to better involve them in enrollment management. They must work with the president to link revenue to expenses to support current and new program initiatives. One area where a good provost can make a difference is in managing facilities design and stakeholder expectations of them. In new or repurposed facilities, the decisions must be taken out of committee-think, where a president can otherwise be forced into the uncomfortable position of telling staff and faculty that the university cannot exceed a limited budget in areas like program development and new construction. In short, the provost manages and enforces priorities developed through a common vision laid out by the president. In this sense, the provost is a kind of political whip, managing expectations and counting votes to remove impediments that preclude execution of an institutional vision.

The chair of the board of trustees is the third member of the senior leadership group. Ideally, board chairs should have extensive experience in higher education, working through various board committees to broaden their higher education experience. For those of us who have served in this job, the most startling revelation is often that our professional work experience elsewhere does not translate into our role as chair. That said, there are three basic skills required. The first is an ability to understand what oversight means on a college campus. The second is a need to use the skills that emerge from the liberal arts tool kit—the ability to speak and write clearly and convincingly; understand nonprofit budgets, debt, and endowments; embrace technology; and work in a collaborate setting—to manage oversight. The third is to be a good listener and an imaginative and thoughtful partner to the president and provost, while maintaining a cordial relationship with the faculty and staff.[26]

Board chairs have three duties: general oversight, approving budgets, and supporting the president. They need to lead trustees through large issues that affect direction and policy, focusing on budgets, audit, and the endowment. Oversight does not involve weighing in on personnel or divisional and department program changes—unless they have a significant impact on the budget—but deciding major questions such as: Should the institution create a new college of nursing? Does analysis from throughout the campus support construction of a new science building? Should the college use third-party financing rather than debt to construct new student residence facilities? The second duty of the board chair is to approve the budget. Boards must look at critical indicators to determine what's possible by carefully monitoring tuition increases, financial aid discounts, level of debt, depreciation, and labor costs. The infamous and famously unnecessary climbing wall is built on a campus only when boards greenlight capital construction projects. Finally, board chairs must be skilled partners to presidents, whom they help select, nurture, support, defend, and replace, when necessary.[27]

Put another way, board chairs are specialists in macro issues that shape policy, hopefully linked to a dynamic strategic vision grounded in financial analysis. The best board chairs ingest all things pertaining to higher education because they must join with the president to translate the world beyond the college gates to the campus.[28] What are the three or four key issues on which the board should concentrate that might become existential threats to the institution? How can committee work be streamlined to focus on these issues? How does the board execute its leadership responsibilities? Is the board transparent in its actions, devoid of clique-like mentality, and the embodiment of the mission that defines the institution? Board chairs should be keenly aware of their limitations and what they do not know.

The first place they should start is with the board itself. Often over-weighted by alumni chosen from among old friends in a few select reunion classes, board chairs must constantly review the effectiveness of how boards govern themselves. Is the board too large to be effective? Is wealth given an outsize voice in policy decisions? Does the board's oversight grow in tandem with an institution that is evolving under a strategic plan to a more sustainable place? The key is that the board chair must manage the relationships among trustees, administrators, and faculty, which is quite different from simply managing the board.[29] To do so, board chairs must be intelligent, thoughtful communicators who place the interests of the institution above their preconceived notions of what a board chair should be. While the responsibilities, especially in management, are considerable, the best board chairs set their egos aside and appreciate that board governance is not a social science experiment or a business case study. The board, not the institution, is theirs to manage.

When the trustees are the weakest link in the chain of shared governance, the board chair takes on a make-or-break significance for the institution. With responsibilities in governance and oversight, good board chairs should steer clear of operations. They must also enforce a separation between the trustees and senior staff and faculty, especially since many of the trustees have long-standing alumni ties to the institution. If these separations are not assiduously maintained, they can significantly weaken and undermine the president, provost, and senior staff. The best board chairs are mindful of day-to-day management and budgets, but they can be instrumental in pushing an agenda, in cooperation with the president, by embracing and enforcing, through management practice, the use of the board's time.

While we could have written separate books on these three leadership roles, our purpose is to illuminate the difference among them, most notably, how they function in shared governance. As we examine functions and processes, these leaders will become critical actors in the success or failure of the institution. In a period of substantial upheaval in American higher education, the dominating question must be how a higher education institution can become more sustainable and thrive when the playbook developed in the last century no longer holds the answer to how to lead a college successfully. Great leadership supports creativity that makes colleges and universities adaptable enough to survive and become sustainable. It is just not easy to find the strategic visionaries to meet the challenges and opportunities ahead.

College leaders should be keenly aware that the world is changing around them. The collapse of the tuition-driven revenue model suggests that the roles and relationships between presidents, provosts, and board chairs will evolve in undetermined ways in a post-pandemic world. Specifically, board chairs will be cultivated and chosen by the board to manage how state, federal, and accrediting requirements shift and intensify, handle escalating competition across higher education, and address faculty and staff concerns about how change affects them. Presidents will become more strategic, relying heavily upon senior staff, provosts, and faculty leadership's ability to translate the need for the campus to become more adaptable—to integrate academic and student life programs, faculty and staff retraining, advocacy and support, new personnel hires, and facilities' needs. The provost's job will be even more difficult as tensions rise, principally over how the operating budget is grown and rationed. But there can also be a silver lining. The established rules of engagement are inadequate to face the challenges of a post-pandemic world. Success and sustainability going forward will be measured by the ability of college and university leaders to reimagine how they think, not only about their roles, but also about each other.

2

Strategic Planning

S trategic planning may be the most misunderstood and derided processes in academic administration. Indeed, many critics argue the sheer uselessness of not only the plan but also the process. At best, critics argue that strategic financial planning, scenario analysis, or comprehensive budgeting might be a better use of time and resources. We strenuously disagree with all of these notions. They fundamentally and dangerously misunderstand or misconstrue the role of strategy in academic planning and management. Strategy is not some overly complicated process for planning and budgeting. Strategy is not a kumbaya moment, when constituents come together and agree. Strategy is not something that is memorialized and resigned to some dusty bookshelf. Strategy and effective strategic planning are none of these things.

The *Oxford English Dictionary* defines strategy as "the art or practice of planning the future direction or outcome of something; the formulation or implementation of a plan, scheme, or course of action, especially of a long-term or ambitious nature."[1] Our three types of president—the presider, the change agent, and the strategic visionary—

are useful to examine in the light of developing and implementing strategy, because the outcome is pivotal to the success or failure of the plan and, ultimately, the institution.

The presider presidents tend toward conservatism. That is never more so than during an omnibus strategic planning process. They will likely insist upon the most representative and inclusive committee structure, utilizing an external consultant as facilitator, a slow and deliberate process, exhaustive rounds of information sessions and community feedback, and finally, approval and adoption from the trustees, faculty, and many other constituencies. While there is nothing wrong with this conservative approach, it often confuses planning for strategy. Roger Martin observes, "I must have heard the words 'we need to create a strategic plan' at least an order of magnitude more times than I have heard 'we need to create a strategy.' This is because most people see strategy as an exercise in producing a planning document. In this conception, strategy is manifested as a long list of initiatives with time frames associated and resources assigned."[2] If the goal of strategic planning is indeed to develop a strategy, then by definition, the resulting plan must present a future direction or outcome of identifiable and measurable success and significance.

Change-agent presidents often have a diametric approach, which favors a faster, more streamlined process. This might take the form of a smaller committee, fewer meetings, less community involvement, a chair instead of a facilitator, a set of questions or directives, a minimal approval process. While this will likely speed up the process, it will also potentially undermine its legitimacy. For a change agent who cannot resist putting his or her thumb on the scale, this is even more of a danger. The change agent wants to make substantial moves and is looking for a strategic plan that allows this to happen. It is often less about the strategy or the plan, and more about presidential initiatives. If this is the case, the president would likely be more successful stating these initiatives outright and separate from the strategy. If done openly, the goals of the strategic plan and the presidential initiatives might be complementary and have a chance of both succeeding.

Strategic-visionary presidents are all about the strategy. They utilize strategic planning to not only generate and agree upon the strategy and associated planning but also to drive the principals through a process of understanding and analysis of the underlying factors. The process will have more in common with that of the presider, especially when it comes to facilitation, representation, and consultation. However, it will likely diverge in the underlying study and analysis. Resneck Pierce writes, "Many planning processes fail because those involved have been encouraged to 'Blue Sky It' without grounding their planning in a clearly-articulated vision for the future and without tethering it to in-depth, cost-benefit analyses and a realistic financial plan . . . It is a recipe for disaster when those involved in planning are asked to imagine a rosy future without regard to available resources: human, financial, and facilities."[3] The strategic visionary is striving for a plan that is strategically significant but also a process that thoroughly educates the committee along the way. This produces a situation of broad ownership of the strategy, the plan, and the institution as it truly exists, warts and all, as a snapshot in time.

Strategy is most typically associated with military leadership and martial actions. In *On War*, Carl von Clausewitz says that strategy "must be compressed into the fewest possible actions—again, ideally, into one. Finally, all minor actions must be subordinated as much as possible. In short the first principle is: act with the utmost concentration."[4] These tenets have been adopted by and incorporated into modern management theory. Martin notes that strategy "is not planning—it is the making of an integrated set of choices that collectively position the firm in its industry so as to create sustainable advantage relative to competition."[5] Both are useful perspectives in thinking about academic strategy and especially when leading the institution through a strategic planning process.

It is also important to differentiate strategy from tactics. Tactics are actions taken to reach a desired end. Thus, many tactical actions will be required to execute any given strategy. Returning to Clausewitz, "tactics and strategy are two activities mutually permeating each other in time and space, at the same time essentially different activities, the inner laws and mutual relations of which cannot be intelligible at all to the mind until a clear conception of the nature of each activity is established."[6] All too often, strategic planning gets consumed with the mechanics of potential implementation. These mechanics have nothing to do with the strategy itself, and they must not be allowed to dominate the discussion. Different strategies must be considered and debated on their own merits. Once the plan is complete, the leadership will be charged with the tactical execution of goals.

When developing a strategic plan, the college or university leadership has several key decisions to make up front. The most important consideration is the role of the president, provost, and board chair in the process. As always, the provost most clearly represents the faculty and their interests, and the board chair does likewise for the trustees. The president is the nexus for all of these interests. Therefore, we argue that the president must head the planning process and ultimately its implementation. That does not mean that the provost and board chair are not equally involved; each has a critical role to play in choosing committee members from his or her associated constituency and in communicating with these constituencies during and after the planning process.

Unfortunately, there is no Platonic perfection when it comes to the composition and functioning of a strategic planning committee. Most would agree that the board, faculty, administration, staff, students, alumni, and community should be represented. However, the form and nature of this representation is usually left up to the leadership. The final composition often comes down to balancing representation with size. Both are important to the successful functioning of the committee. However, accommodations may need to be made. For example, members may be chosen to more broadly represent constituencies. The chair of the faculty senate, alumni association president, and student government president are often selected for this reason. Nevertheless, alternative voices and diversity need to be considered as well. This is especially important if the institution has known challenges that differentially affect certain constituencies. The leadership is wise to make these decisions in a transparent and deliberate manner.

The chairing of the committee and facilitation of its work are also best considered up front. These choices will determine the timely functioning and resulting product of the committee's work. We recommend that the president serve as chair. Our reasoning is twofold. First, the president will ultimately be held responsible for the success or failure of the strategic plan. Second, the president must orchestrate the implementation of the plan in continuing relationships with the many constituent bodies. Therefore, the president should assume this leadership role from the beginning. As for facilitation, it is often wise to engage an outside consultant in addition to the chair of the committee. This facilitator is chosen based on demonstrated objectivity, knowledge of the planning process, and ability to bring competing or conflicting interests into alignment. She or he will shepherd the process. This work may be completely new to some of the participants. While others may have more experience, it is unlikely that most of the committee will have the breadth of strategic planning experience that a professional facilitator brings. In addition to experience, it is helpful to have someone who can record and synthesize the committee's work. As the plan coalesces, the facilitator often works to resolve any remaining differences. Ultimately, the goal is to produce a plan that has broad committee support.

Any consideration of academic strategy begins and ends with the mission of the institution. The first task of the committee is to review the mission (and associated vision, if there is one). Any strategic ideas considered by the committee must fit within this mission. If the committee cannot agree upon this premise from the beginning, then the work should likely begin with a reconsideration of the mission. While this is not a prescription for expediency, it may be necessary if the mission has become outdated or outmoded. Once the committee agrees upon the mission, the strategic work can begin.

Ipsa scientia potestas est (knowledge itself is power).[7] This is never truer than for the purpose of developing strategy. Therefore, any strategic planning process that proceeds without a thorough review of the institution and the competitive environment will be fundamentally flawed. Like discussing the mission, this step may seem tedious and is often ignored. The committee will likely be more inclined to start pitching big hairy audacious goals.[8] There will be a time for brain-storming, but it comes after this necessary step. This process, how-ever, does not need to be as tedious as it sounds. It can be a time of reflection on the true state of the institution, which includes the entire community. The act of gathering, analyzing, and synthesizing this information can be a reassuring grounding for both the committee and the community. In fact, this is a good opportunity to begin the process in total transparency. Most of the information can be shared, and it opens a discussion about strategic opportunities. All of this provides the necessary realism, both about the institution and its peers for the committee to study and consider. In fact, many institutions look back on this step as pivotal to the success of the resulting strategy and plan.

Anyone who has stared at a blank page or canvas knows the thrill and trepidation of beginning the creative process. The crafting of strategy is no different. In a limited amount of time, the committee must go from "the sky is the limit" to a manageable set of defined strategic goals. While it may seem wide open, the options may be constrained in a variety of ways. First, the time frame of the plan naturally limits what can be accomplished. A ten-year plan will look very different from a three-year plan, even at the same organization. Second, the existing state of the college or university will play heavily into the implementation. That is why it is so important for the committee to know these details at the beginning of the process. Third, budgetary constraints will also play heavily into the planning. The committee must be realistic about what financial resources will be available and about the institution's overriding financial goals (e.g., a balanced budget). While fundraising can and often does partially finance the implementation, it, too, has its limitations. These must be considered in the planning process, otherwise the resulting strategy and goals will be unattainable. Finally, the leadership may choose to focus more on one domain than another. This will also guide the committee's work.[9]

Once the constraints have been defined, the planning process may begin in earnest. If the institution has enlisted the services of a facilitator, he or she usually brings a proposed process to the work. Of course, with or without a facilitator, the committee may want to define its own process. In either case, it will begin with information gathering and brainstorming. The committee may find this process too open-ended, even with proper constraints. This is when innovation systems and tools for group thinking may be helpful. The author (King) began his career using innovation systems at Hughes and Disney, both companies known for their creative and innovative environments. At Disney, Task writes, "Walt Disney wore three different hats when he engaged in his work: the Creative, the Critic, and the Planner. Disney would literally dress and act differently when he was in each role, and coworkers could identify which Disney had shown up at that day's meeting."[10] The brainstorming happens in creative mode, where there are no bad ideas. The critical and planning modes are the crucible. Planning determines how something can be achieved. However, it may determine that an idea cannot be achieved (at least, not within the constraints). Criticism is much more subjective, but equally important. It is where ideas and plans are refined or even rejected. However, each of these three processes must be given room to work independently. Nothing will stop brainstorming in its tracks like criticism.

There are more generally available tools and systems for creative thinking and group discussions that might also be useful. Edward de Bono's system is based on "six thinking hats," which symbolically embody different mental processes. The White Hat seeks information. The Yellow Hat looks for value and benefits. The Red Hat examines the emotional and intuitive. The Green Hat focuses on possibilities, alternatives, and new ideas. The Black Hat is critical, exposing flaws and weaknesses. The Blue Hat manages the thinking process, specifically making sure that the processes are in balance.[11] The design company IDEO has a process of "design thinking" that balances desirability, viability, and feasibility. It uses a process of divergent and convergent thinking to develop ideas through three core activities: inspiration, ideation, and implementation.[12] All of these systems and processes are designed to lead the group through a process of iteration toward a goal.

If all goes well, the process will conclude with a plan that neatly encapsulates a singular strategy broken into an achievable set of goals. It should not be a laundry list of ideas, a monumental collection of audacious (and unachievable) goals, a Christmas tree with presents for everyone, or milquetoast platitudes. It should be a set of goals that can reasonably and demonstrably improve the institution in its performance of the mission. These goals may be holistic or further broken into sub-goals. However, they should not be overly prescriptive or tactical. As discussed previously, the implementation should be left to administration working in concert with the faculty, staff, and trustees.

Once the plan is complete, it must go through an approval process to legitimize the process and the resulting plan. Institutions often struggle with the inclusiveness of this approval process. Many constituents expect it to be as broad as the initial conversations about the state of the institution and potential strategic opportunities. While this expectation is understandable, it is also misguided and can create real problems. The governors of the institution, namely, the trustees and faculty, must approve the plan. Some institutions may go one step further and include a staff resolution, based on the historical inclusion of the staff in such processes. However, even this can be problematic if the implementation of the plan has negative consequences for the staff. The trustees and faculty own the strategy because they are corporately responsible for it. The administration is charged with executing it, and the president's performance will be assessed by the board in that regard. None of the other constituent bodies bear this authority or responsibility. All of this can and should be disclosed in a transparent manner early in the process.

The adoption of the plan may seem like the end to the committee, but for most of the institution, it is just the beginning. The leadership will feel some pressure to get under way, especially if the time frame is short. Nevertheless, the next few steps can mean the difference between success and failure. It is the process of turning the strategy and its goals into operations and tactics. The process may be more or less straightforward, depending on the plan itself. If the goals are easily categorized as academic affairs, student life, advancement, etc., then the divvying up of responsibilities may be relatively easy. However, if the goals cut across institutional units, the process of dividing the work and responsibility may be quite a bit more complicated, and working groups may be a more appropriate structure for managing the implementation. The key is making sure that each goal is properly assigned and monitored throughout the implementation process.

The next step is to consider tactics. The strategy and goals may be approached in any number of ways. Tactically, is it better to sequence them in a certain order? How should resources be brought to bear? Is the necessary expertise internal to the institution? Where do we anticipate the least and most resistance? Have other colleges and universities done it? If so, how? If not, has it been done in other industries? These sorts of tactical questions will likely determine both the expediency and degree of success. Building a tactical plan associated with each goal helps the group responsible to truly understand the goal and its "moving parts." This process also allows the group to go from macro to micro. Big goals spread out over years have to be divided into stages, assigned to the appropriate people, monitored through the execution, and finally assessed. Success requires careful management, spread across months or years.

Another avenue that is often ignored is a serious environmental scan. This is the process of methodically researching the strategies, goals, structures, curriculum, programs, and methods of implementation at other colleges and universities, both peers and non-peers. Implementing a strategic plan is not a time for myopia when it comes to institutional uniqueness. "Until I left a college presidency and joined the Mellon Foundation, I did not fully appreciate how many colleges and universities really do see themselves as 'unique'—and as 'truly unique' when it comes to fundable ideas . . . Colleges seldom look for connections with other institutions; they feel comfortable competing for strategic advantage in terms of students, faculty, academic distinction, fundraising, and grants in the belief that all relevant expertise and experience can be found on one's own campus," observes Eugene Tobin.[13] Clearly, this is a mistake, and such narrowmindedness does not befit an academic institution. It is incumbent upon the leadership not to allow this to occur.

Other factors will also play into the successful execution of the plan. First, the college or university must be aware of its accreditor. Most accreditors require some sort of institutional improvement or quality enhancement as a part of their reaffirmation process. For example, the Higher Learning Commission has an option for a specific Academic Quality Improvement Plan (AQIP), which "is focused on quality assurance and institutional improvement, but with an added emphasis on helping institutions achieve continuous quality improvement."[14] While this option has decreased in popularity and is being phased out, the principles will likely be integrated into their other reaffirmation pathways. Alternately, the Southern Association of Colleges and Schools requires a Quality Enhancement Plan (QEP) as a part of their decennial review. The purpose of the QEP is "to enhance overall institutional quality and effectiveness by focusing on an issue that the institution considers important to improving student learning outcomes and/or student success."[15] In any case, it is not unlikely that the institution's strategic plan will intersect or embody plans required by the accreditor. This should be considered throughout the planning and implementation process.

"Sunlight is said to be the best of disinfectants," Louis Brandeis famously noted.[16] When it comes to transparency on campus, it is almost impossible to have too much. Certainly, there are real needs for confidentiality in regard to student records, human resources, executive actions, etc. However, this is a small, well-defined set. Almost everything else can be disclosed at some level of specificity and timeliness. This is an important consideration as the strategic plan is being developed, implemented, and assessed. At an institution that has a strong commitment to transparency, the strategic plan is no different from anything else. However, at colleges and universities that have struggled with transparency, the strategic plan provides a rare opportunity. Transparency can be built into the planning process from the beginning. If done well, no one will be left wondering how the proverbial sausage was made. The same goes for the execution of the plan. In fact, every stage can be useful in building and reinforcing transparency. For the administration and board of trustees, the benefits can be significant, but the greater beneficiary is the institution. It could mean the difference between success and failure of the strategic plan.

Another major consideration during and after the planning process is momentum. Visionary processes often create their own momentum, but it is a mistake to assume that this will happen. It is incumbent upon the leadership to set the pace and drive the momentum. During the planning, this can be done by simply laying out a timeline and sticking to it. The years-long rollout is a much greater concern. However, the goals provide a natural structure for defining a marketing and communications plan that celebrates the completion of discrete steps and maintains momentum. When this is done for each goal, the differing implementation timelines actually contribute to a feeling of steady strategic progress. Another consideration is the detractors or, in the social-media world, the haters. These voices can be expected to ebb and flow throughout, but there are certain predictable points of friction. The beginning and end of the planning process are likely targets, as well as the major milestones of each of the goals. With effective preparation, there is no reason for the institution or leadership to be caught off guard at any of these points. The communication program in its entirety should be considered a component of the educational process for the many constituencies previously discussed.

It is not unusual for the strategic plan to intersect the planning of the campus. "A campus master plan is a physical manifestation of a university's strategic plan. At its best, it is a road map for the future of a campus, and becomes a crucial tool in confirming that short-term projects are working in conjunction with long-term plans and goals," states Virginia Tech's planning and construction website.[17] Many strategic plans do not make overt mention of facilities. It is the associated master planning process that does the analysis and puts the pieces in place. "Without it, each decision made about a campus' facilities—from new buildings to renovations to infrastructure improvements—is made in isolation, without a bigger vision in mind. And a good campus plan builds in flexibility, so that it can accommodate shifting academic priorities and economic conditions," Virginia Tech's facilities department goes on to explain.[18] Of course, master plans can influence the entire direction of the institution and its strategy.

Thomas Jefferson did a great deal of thinking about the location and physical campus when he began laying out plans for what would become the University of Virginia. In fact, his earliest letters about the university referenced this thinking. In January 1800, Jefferson wrote Dr. Joseph Priestley, the natural philosopher and discoverer of oxygen, "We wish to establish in the upper and healthier country, and more centrally for the state an [sic] University on a plan so broad and liberal and modern, as to be worth patronizing with the public support, and be a temptation to the youth of other states to come, and drink of the cup of knowledge and fraternize with us."[19] He had very specific notions when it came to the campus plan. Writing to Littleton Tazewell, a Virginia lawyer and politician, in 1805, he asserted that "large houses are always ugly, inconvenient, exposed to the accident of fire, and bad in cases of infection. A plain small house for the school and lodging of each professor is best. These connected by covered ways out of which the rooms of the students should open would be best. These may then be built only as they shall be wanting. In fact, an [sic] University should not be an [sic] house but a village."[20] By 1810, Jefferson's thinking had solidified into a master plan that one would recognize touring the modern University of Virginia. He wrote to another correspondent, "the whole arranged around an open square of grass and trees would make it, what it should be in fact, an academical village."[21] This division of disciplines into separate buildings and an associated curriculum that allowed for intellectual curiosity and self-direction in the program of study presaged the modern research university. In a very real sense, Jefferson's master plan for the University of Virginia set the course of its strategic evolution.

While few master plans or strategic plans will have such a long-lasting effect, any one of them very well could. It is important that academic leaders understand this and the gravity of the visioning process. It should be in the mind of every president, provost, and board chair. It should inform his or her leadership of and participation in the process. There is a specific role for each of these leaders to play. Ownership should be taken by all three, but there is no more important ownership than that taken by the president. In a very real sense, this will be their legacy at the institution. However, it is vitally important that the many constituents involved in the strategic planning process feel equal degrees of ownership. This is where the provost and board chair can play key roles.

Provosts know the mood and pulse of the faculty. They know their concerns and flashpoints, their predilections and aversions. Even the smallest of faculties have a broad range of voices, decades of interaction as colleagues, and strong interests and desires when it comes to the institution. In fact, they often have the longest and most intimate histories with the institution. That is why the strategic planning process is most personal to the faculty. The provost should advise and guide the selection of faculty for the strategic planning committee and any working groups or subcommittees assigned to it. This work will often involve balancing different faculty interests, along with the interests of the administration and trustees. It can be a very delicate process. If it is not done well, the process and resulting plan will not have the legitimacy that is critical for its success. Therefore, it is arguably the most critical role that the provost plays in the strategic planning process, and thus it should be performed assiduously. It is not the only role, however. The provost and the academic affairs staff also provide deep insight into and analysis of the curriculum, assessment process, and outcomes. They have a broader knowledge of other institutions, which they can interject into the conversation. Finally, they have experience implementing plans, which is very useful in defining and scoping the goals.

The board chair plays an analogous role with the trustees. Like the faculty, trustees often have a long and intimate history with the institution, as students, athletes, alumni, parents, boosters, major donors. The older trustees may fondly remember a college or university that bears little resemblance to the modern institution. This nostalgia is understandable, but it must be balanced with the current and future needs of the institution. This is accomplished by carefully choosing the trustees on the strategic planning committee. The board chair likely has the best sense of the individual trustees. Working with the president, he or she can determine how each should be engaged with the process. Certainly, there will be trustees chosen to sit directly on the committee. However, this is not the only avenue for participation. The trustees on the committee will likely represent different functions of the board, such as finance, advancement, or facilities. This allows for more voices to be heard, while still maintaining a manageable and balanced committee as a whole.

In times of crisis, best practices may come into conflict with urgency. The temptation will be to compress time frames and limit representation. This may indeed be necessary, but it should be done with great care and with constrained purview. The resulting plan should address the crisis and no more. It may then be replaced with a more thoughtful solution later on; this sunset clause provision can even be included in the original charge to assuage concerns about the process. Except for dire circumstances, this sort of planning should not be used to make strategic decisions. It is better to defer these decisions to the holistic, inclusive, and deliberate process described in this chapter. Leadership should take special care not to leverage (or worse, manufacture) a crisis to drive the planning process, because it will undermine trust in equal measure.

Not all strategic planning processes occur in a centralized, top-down structure. Innovation and brainstorming can be seeded in a bottom-up fashion. For example, Whitman College developed its Diversity Innovation Grants to "enable faculty to enhance learning experiences for students that will better equip them for life in a rapidly changing multicultural world with particular attention to issues of power, privilege, and difference."[22] These modest $4,000 and $8,000 grants encourage experimentation and collaboration while focusing on an important strategic issue. This generative activity can drive the most successful ideas through iterative refinement and ultimately percolate them up to the strategic planning process itself. This activity can be built into the process from the beginning, recognizing that good ideas are often generated organically, not through deliberate organizational structures and procedures.

As noted earlier in this chapter, once the planning process is complete, the plan must be approved by the trustees and faculty. This process will involve president, board chair, and provost working in concert to shepherd the final plan through the shared governance process. This step is crucial and must be treated as such. It is not a time to rush or circumvent. On the contrary, it is essential that great care be taken in the completion of this task. If slightly more reflection or feedback is helpful, it should be encouraged. A stumble at the end of the process can impede momentum or, worse, challenge legitimacy. Alternately, a graceful and celebratory completion can set the course for success more than almost anything else. It is a time for the shared governors to proudly look to the future and embark on the journey together. This combined vision and optimism will drive much that comes afterward. It will likely have great bearing on the success of an associated capital campaign and on the communications required to engage the many constituencies in the execution of the plan. In short, it is a time for leadership.

3

Management and Operations

The Great Recession and its demographic aftermath have put extraordinary financial strain on colleges and universities. The COVID-19 pandemic and resulting economic displacement have greatly exacerbated these problems, causing an ongoing emphasis on finances, especially revenue, at many institutions. Senior management in enrollment, advancement, and business and finance have taken on much greater institutional responsibility. This is a natural response to the changing climate, but it presents a challenge to institutional leaders. They must cultivate better managers internally or seek them externally, in an increasingly competitive environment. They must also work hard to hang on to talent. This begins with understanding the different roles and the stresses and burdens that each must bear. We think that thoughtful leaders would be well served by a careful examination of the challenges faced by each role and operational unit.

The modern vice president for enrollment management is in a much different position from the twentieth-century dean of admission. From social media boosting to stagnant median family income, the challenges of modern enrollment management begin with the students and families that the institution serves. The market has changed dramatically within the last decade. "It increasingly resembles the rest of the commercial world, in which come-ons relentlessly pelt consumers' skulls, incentives drive decisions, and everyone expects to bargain. Here's a 40-percent-off promo code! We will not be undersold! Act now—this special offer expires soon!," writes Eric Hoover.[1] This change was driven in part by the US Justice Department's investigations of admissions scandals in 2019.[2] The scope of the inquiry quickly expanded to industry standards, specifically, the code of ethics long observed by the National Association for College Admission Counseling (NACAC) and its members. Portions of this code were deemed anticompetitive, and NACAC removed them, rather than face formal scrutiny and potential legal action by the government.[3]

Under the revised code of ethics, colleges and universities no longer have to observe May 1 as National Decision Day for regular-decision applicants. They can aggressively solicit decisions and deposits from the moment they admit the student. Of course, so can every other institution that has admitted the student. Hoover describes the new dynamic: "In mid-January, a college applicant in the suburbs of Chicago received an enticing offer. It came from an admissions counselor at Illinois Wesleyan University, who left him a voicemail message and followed up with a text. 'You have been selected,' the text said, 'to receive an extra $2,000 per year in scholarship money!'" There was one stipulation. Because funds were limited, the university would hold the offer for just two weeks. "If you deposit by February 1st," the text said, "then you are guaranteed the extra 2k. Let me know if you have any questions!" Later that day, the young man shared the news with Augustana College, in Rock Island, Illinois, which had sent him a financial-aid package several weeks earlier. "Could Augustana, he asked, match Illinois Wesleyan's latest offer? He needed an answer by February 1 . . . [Augustana] didn't hesitate to increase the Chicago student's aid award."[4] In a single enrollment season, higher education, as an industry, had gone from anticompetitive to hypercompetitive. A code of ethics that had endured for generations was compromised. According to an EAB survey, 23 percent of enrollment vice presidents say they will consider recruiting students who have already committed to another institution. For schools with enrollments below one thousand, 54 percent said they would be willing to poach.[5]

This willingness to undercut competitors changes not just the annual enrollment cycle but also the transfer cycle. NACAC had very strict guidelines regarding transfers: "Colleges will not knowingly recruit . . . students who are already enrolled at other institutions," and "colleges must not solicit transfer applications from a previous year's applicant or prospect pool."[6] Both of these provisions were struck from the NACAC code of ethics. It is not hard to imagine institutions circling back to students who chose to go elsewhere with a new financial aid package or other incentive to transfer. However, the tactics could quickly become far more aggressive. Imagine an enrollment team from another institution arriving on your campus to recruit transfer students. A private institution would have the ability to enforce its property rights, but a public institution would have little recourse other than to appeal to the professional integrity of the interlopers. While these scenarios might be a bit extreme, it is not hard to see why enrollment officers are worried.

In a 2019 *Inside Higher Ed* survey of admissions directors, more than half reported that their institution had not hit its enrollment goals by July 1.[7] Most said that they were concerned about hitting their new student enrollment goals. Most also believe that their institution is losing potential applicants due to concerns about student debt. Finally, most agree that higher education needs to do a better job explaining the value of earning a college degree. A majority are concerned about maintaining their enrollment of international students, and they also report seeking more out-of-state students in recent years. A majority also thinks that the year's admissions scandals have hurt the images of colleges and universities implicated, as well as harming the integrity and fairness of the admissions process at US colleges.[8] These worries and the associated burnout are driving unprecedented turnover in enrollment leadership.[9] Angel Pérez, Vice President for Enrollment and Student Success at Trinity College, writes, "Most people who inherit the role were trained as admissions officers, a job that rarely provides adequate preparation for the diverse responsibilities of today's enrollment manager. I am expected to serve as an institutional leader who attracts talented students from across the globe and helps them finance their education, all while using the latest research and high-impact practices to create models for student success and outcomes. I must achieve all of this while meeting the college's revenue and student-demographic goals."[10]

Advancement leadership faces equally daunting challenges and expectations, at a time when colleges and universities are turning to giving to relieve pressure from enrollment. St. John's College, in Annapolis, Maryland, and Santa Fe, New Mexico, began a $300 million capital campaign in 2018.[11] The purpose of the campaign is to relieve pressure on enrollment for net tuition revenue. "Today, most families read one message in these astronomical sticker prices: You cannot come here," states the campaign prospectus.[12] It continues, "The time has come for colleges to make a transformational change around college affordability and transparency, and St. John's is taking the lead in redefining the financial model."[13] The campaign intends to increase the existing $197 million endowment by $200 million. In doubling the endowment, the annual draw will fund 65 percent of financial aid. In FY2016, only 18 percent of financial aid was funded by the endowment. The college also intends raise $50 million in annual contributions to support operations until the endowment contributions are collected.[14] Gordon College received a $75.5 million lead gift in their $130 million campaign.[15] It was designated for the endowment to fund scholarships. The annual draw will have an immediate impact. Funded financial aid will increase by 15 percent in the fall of 2020. However, it is the rare college or university that has a donor base with this degree of capacity. For most institutions, the annual fund is directed toward funding financial aid, and the annual fund is primarily driven by alumni.

Unfortunately, alumni participation has been dropping for decades. Dan Allenby notes that "in 1990, 18 percent of college and university alumni gave to their alma mater, according to the Council for

Aid to Education. By 2013, that number had been cut in half to less than 9 percent—a record low and a culmination of a trend that has persisted for more than two decades."[16] In 2019, only eighty-four colleges and universities had alumni participation rates of 20 percent or higher.[17] The Council for the Advancement and Support of Education (CASE) urges alumni support to be viewed more broadly. It may include volunteer engagement, such as board service, mentoring, and guest speaking. Alternately, communication engagement, especially on social media, can create a strong community bond with the alma mater, driven primarily by alumni communications and dialogue.[18] These may not directly generate giving, but they can certainly generate a positive environment in which to solicit funds from more capable donors. In that regard, recent trends are more positive. In 2018, total contributions to higher education increased 7.2 percent, to almost $47 billion. In fact, charitable contributions to colleges and universities reached the highest levels ever recorded, according to a CASE survey.[19] Unfortunately, this largesse is not evenly distributed. Many institutions will not have donor capacity or donor willingness at a level capable of blunting the effects of enrollment shortfalls.

The chief business officer is probably more aware of these realities than anyone else on the leadership team. In a 2019 *Inside Higher Ed* survey, only half of these officers were confident that their college or university would be financially stable over the next ten years.[20] Most of the business officers surveyed believed that additional colleges will close, with a third expecting more than ten closures in the coming year. Most think that there will be additional private and public college and university mergers.[21] This is certainly not an optimistic outlook. The chief business officer (CBO) is often more worried than anyone about the stiff headwinds that face higher education. Because of this, they are in a unique position to address the situation. "The role of the CBO has always been quite broad, often with responsibility for all aspects of finance, human resources, facilities, auxiliary services, information technology, campus police, and risk management," note Thomas Ayers and Karen Goldstein.[22] However, the role has expanded in recent years.

Whether it is styled as CBO or CFO or vice president for business and finance, the position has become more of a catalyst for strategic conversations and planning around financial constraints and contingencies, as well as changes in the marketplace.

This mirrors the changing nature of the role in American corporations. Kasia Moreno observes, "Today's CFO is managing an ecosystem of expanding complexity—thinking and operating [holistically], leveraging financial data and analytics, challenging and enabling business strategies and capitalizing on a shifting regulatory environment—all with a view to achieving competitive advantage. CFOs are looking beyond their traditional finance role to become more collaborative and insightful business partners boosting the relevance and value they contribute to the business."[23] Don Mailliard, an executive at KPMG, calls this the Renaissance CFO. "Renaissance CFOs need to manage capital, of course, but they also need to be versed in strategy, in analytics, in operations, and in talent management. In short, they need to help drive business change. It's a daunting task, but it isn't out of reach."[24] Higher education is probably more desperate for change than most industries, given the demographic and cost challenges it faces. A substantial part of this change will be data driven. "While once management reporting was 80 percent gathering information and 20 percent analyzing it, automation means that ratio can be flipped, putting more of a focus on understanding the data instead of just reporting it," writes Mailliard.[25] This is certainly true for colleges and universities. They have access not only to their own data but also to enormous amounts of peer data through the Integrated Postsecondary Education Data System (IPEDS) and other repositories. With the rich technology infrastructure on most campuses, new sources of data are becoming routinely available.

Aaron Benz founded Degree Analytics to utilize real-time network data to track students on campus via their mobile devices.[26] In addition to tracking class attendance, such a system can monitor all sorts of activity: library utilization, time spent in one's room, social events, etc. There are certainly serious privacy considerations that need to be balanced with this utility, and frankly, to avoid creating an Orwellian campus community. However, Benz's intentions were based on his own college experience:

> I was diagnosed with Hodgkins Lymphoma [and] started receiving chemo treatments shortly after. I thought I could still go to college and receive chemo at the same time. I really had no business attending college that semester and certainly no business attending one that was 11 hours away from home. If it were left to my own devices, I would have dropped out. My success had basically nothing to do with me and essentially everything to do with the people around me. I had professors who personally sought out a relationship to make sure I could keep up with the work—proactively making themselves available for classes I had to miss. I had teammates who stayed in the dorm with me on Halloween after a treatment instead of having fun with everyone else. I had parents and coaches and friends and strangers who monitored, cared for, and acted where they could. They wouldn't allow me to fail. I didn't have an opportunity to do anything else but succeed.[27]

With new analytic tools and technologies, data-driven and data-informed decision-making is reaching a new level of sophistication. This challenges the leadership, especially the business and finance officer, to utilize these capabilities at least as effectively as other industries do.

Given all of these challenges, capabilities, complexities, and nuances, a new president must consider the "terms of engagement." The president must assume the leadership role that she or he was assigned from the outset. This can be tricky with institutionalists, especially in the cabinet, who see the president as an inexperienced, unqualified, or transitory figure—the wait- him-or-her-out problem. The type of president will have a significant effect on this early stage. The presider is apt to utilize the existing leadership staff and structures, minimizing the friction of change. Their approach to the governance structures of the institution will usually follow a similar status quo approach. Any change will be a slow and deliberate process, usually after much discussion and deliberation. While some may find this frustrating, there is a compelling logic to the presider's approach. A new president is unlikely to grasp the underlying political and social dynamics of the existing leadership and governance structures. Previous experience can often be misleading due to the significant differences between institutions, regions, accreditors, and so on. The presider takes care to study these differences and is aware that their opinions are likely being influenced or courted by senior staff. Therefore, unimpeded judgment may be difficult and determined by opinion, innuendo, and first moves, which are blunted by the presider's earnest, status quo approach.

In stark contrast, the change agent is eager to get things done. This often takes the form of early changes in leadership. The most extreme example is asking the entire cabinet for letters of resignation. While the president may not choose to accept most of them, it gives the change agent broad authority to quickly alter the leadership. The speed and scope of these changes can challenge the usual norms of shared governance and deliberate process. This can substantially abbreviate the "honeymoon period" and consume significant political capital. However, it enables the president to rapidly put in place leadership capable of and willing to enact a sweeping agenda in short order. There are certainly circumstances in which this pace of change may be crucial. The Great Recession and the COVID-19 pandemic both necessitated rapid change in reaction to public health orders, the market downturn, and subsequent effects on enrollment. Involuntary presidential turnover may also create a situation ideally suited for a change agent. Michael Harris and Molly Ellis report that financial controversy and loss of board confidence are the two most likely causes of involuntary turnover.[28] In either case, the next president will likely feel urgent pressure to act. A third of these involuntary turnovers occur in the second and third years of the president's tenure, the causes of which are listed in table 3.1.[29] So, in a real sense, there is an urgency in many college presidencies, whether or not the new president's temperament matches it.

In this vein, the strategic visionary may have the Goldilocks temperament. Good strategy is not developed overnight or in a vacuum. It is developed after a significant listening period and a deliberate and inclusive strategic-planning process. This gives the strategic visionary

Table 3.1. Causes of involuntary presidential turnover, by year of term

Turnover	<1	1	2	3	4	5	6	7	8	9	10	11	12	13	16	Grand total
Financial controversy	2	2	1		3	2	1	1			1	1	1	1		16
Loss of board confidence		1	1	4	2	1	1	1		1		1		1		14
Poor judgment	2	1	2	1	2	2			1		1					12
Athletics controversy			3	2		1	2			1					1	10
Loss of faculty confidence		1		1		1		1	2		1					7
Poor fit		2	3	1												6
Loss of system confidence					1	1	1				1					4
Total	2	7	11	11	5	9	5	3	4	3	3	2	1	2	1	69

Source: Michael S. Harris and Molly K. Ellis, "Exploring Involuntary Presidential Turnover in American Higher Education," *Journal of Higher Education* 89, no. 3 (2018): 10–11.

time to assess members of the senior staff and make necessary changes in an orderly fashion. It also allows time for broad-based searches to be conducted that appropriately engage faculty and staff. These choices are based not only on the evolving strategy but also on the vision that the president brings to the process. She or he will be looking for a cabinet that can work together to synthesize this vision and strategy to advance the mission of the college or university. Senior staff will be called upon to run their particular areas in a way that facilitates this synthesis. In this way, the strategic visionary values harmony more than the other two presidential types and creates a leadership atmosphere that values and drives continuous improvement over status quo or radical change. This management team will naturally be more focused on assessment as a means of measuring progress and effectiveness.

All three presidential styles can be effective, especially in different periods of the evolution and life of a particular institution. However, this effectiveness will be as much a product of operations as management style. Operations may be understood as the translation of management authority into institutional action. The structure and experience of the staff play a substantial role, often more significant than the management itself, in the effectiveness of institutional operations. Even the most expert and efficient of cabinets is captive to the organizational structure and associated staffing. The leadership must earnestly address these structural challenges to achieve maximal effectiveness and success.

The structure of any particular college or university has usually evolved over decades, even centuries, and it may be radically different from that of even close peer institutions. Some of these differences may be purely idiosyncratic, while others may have deep grounding in the institution and be based on longstanding tradition. The challenge for a new president is to develop an understanding of the structure while also managing the enterprise. This understanding must include the shared governors (i.e., trustees and faculty) and the nuanced role each body plays in relation to the institution and staff. This process takes patience and time, during the portion of a presidency when the president has the most political capital. A tension often develops, especially for the change agent, between wanting to listen and wanting to act. The role of listening cannot be overstated. Listening is the natural counterpart to transparency, and it is essential in shared governance. Therefore, a new president is wise to take this task seriously in determining changes to the operational structure that may be required to achieve his or her goals. It is as critical to leadership as the changes themselves.

Structural and staffing adjustments should be an equally measured process. The tradition of collegiality in the academy is paramount to the success of these adjustments. Depending on the nature of the role (e.g., chief academic officer versus chief financial officer), this process will likely be different. Academic affairs positions typically involve current or former faculty members, who will likely transition back to a faculty role within the institution or on to a different institution as either faculty or administration. Maintaining collegiality requires that the individual should be given adequate time and support to gracefully make this transition. Business and finance staff, on the other hand, usually have many more employment options and do not face a prolonged search process. During these adjustments, senior staff may come to their own conclusions about whether they will stay and support the new administration or move on to another institution. Again, fairness and collegiality are important in successfully executing these departures. The president should carefully weigh each change and the resulting structural modifications that may be required or enabled in the process.

Nontraditional presidents often struggle with these changes, to their own detriment. "Non-academic administrators are often viewed with suspicion by faculty. College isn't an oil company or a law firm, they say; a college is supposed to produce knowledge, not profits. Some say these nontraditional college presidents [cut] costs by replacing tenured faculty with low-paid adjuncts—that these outsiders are not familiar with the culture and traditions of academia that prize debate and the full participation of all faculty members," writes Laura McKenna.[30] This is not a new problem. Gen. Dwight D. Eisenhower was elected president of Columbia University is 1948. His only experience in the academy was the four years he spent as a student at West Point. After two years at Columbia, he tendered his resignation, but the trustees refused to accept it. Nevertheless, he left to run the North Atlantic Treaty Organization.[31] "Lacking a broad scholarly background or advanced graduate degrees, Eisenhower constantly felt inferior among Columbia's erudite faculty . . . Eisenhower lacked the time, interest, or patience to learn how to engage effectively with Columbia's faculty, and made little to no effort on that front. Consequently, the gulf widened between Eisenhower and Columbia's academic community, which resulted in considerable faculty resentment toward Eisenhower," observes Sean Heuvel.[32] This is not an indictment of nontraditional presidents, but a recognition of the unique challenges they face.

Once the new president has completed these staffing and structural changes, he or she is ready to make the strategic plan, master plan, and other initiatives operational. This is when political capital and goodwill will be most valuable. If it was squandered in making staffing and structural changes or by simply not listening early on, success will be much more difficult. This is also a time when values and culture can be reaffirmed by decision-making, operations, and even new construction. Frank Lloyd Wright's design for the headquarters of the Larkin

Company, known for its generous corporate culture, notably embedded organizational values into the design of the building. Relief sculptures in the lobby were inscribed, "To Acquire and Cherish: Humility, Knowledge, Strength . . . To Inspire and Diffuse: Ideas, Emotions, Inventions."[33] The building's atrium was similarly adorned with three-word panels, such as "Faith, Hope, Charity" and "Prudence, Learning, Wisdom."[34] The college or university's mission and core values are often memorialized in a similar manner. With a long tradition in the academy (and before that, in the church), these are not mere gestures but a recognition of the exceptional nature of the institution's mission and the devotion of its constituents to that mission.

The financing and execution of the strategic plan is a good example of how operations and corporate structure must work to achieve strategic goals. Many strategic plans are accompanied by capital campaigns to finance the initiatives. This is often a tricky affair since capital campaigns take time to execute and require large swaths of the president's time and energy. They are also a stress test, of sorts, for the management and operations. With the president out raising money, the management team must operate autonomously. They must plan and execute large-scale efforts with minimal guidance. These efforts often reveal structural and leadership issues that need to be resolved.

When the University of Tulsa developed a plan for "reimagining" the institution, there were clearly substantial hurdles to be overcome. This task fell largely to the provost, Janet K. Levit, since the president was primarily occupied with external relations and fundraising.[35] The newly imagined institution was to be "a high-touch undergraduate institution that provides all students with a firm grounding in critical and creative thinking, and that is STEM-heavy with a professional, practical focus."[36] This required major changes to the functioning of the core curriculum. "The restructuring, in which all undergraduates begin in University Studies before selecting a major, is meant to 'punctuate' the liberal arts, [Levit] added, 'to make sure that all of our students, once they arrive, have that common liberal-arts-and-sciences foundation,'" reports Becky Supiano.[37] Changes of this magnitude often have a low likelihood of success, and this case proved to be no exception. Within a year, the faculty passed a vote of no confidence in both the president and provost.[38]

One wonders what management and operational decisions lead to this outcome. Both president and provost were internal candidates. The president had served two years as the health sciences dean. The provost had spent her entire academic career at the institution, serving on the law faculty, as law school dean, and ultimately as provost. They were both intimately familiar with the university's structures, traditions, and personalities. Nevertheless, the faculty felt that they "were not properly included in decision-making and that some of the changes [would] adversely affect TU's reputation and academic rigor."[39] Was this a failure of shared governance? Was it a failure of leadership? These are difficult questions to answer, especially considering the university's ongoing struggle with a substantial structural deficit, despite its sizable endowment. Nevertheless, the institution must find a way to right itself and ultimately reach a financially sustainable state of operations. This is the challenge to be borne by the next president, working with the trustees and faculty. It is incumbent upon him or her to answer the questions posed above. Success depends upon it.

Of course, success may also depend upon studying the process of successful restructurings and reorganizations at other institutions. Gary Olson, provost at Idaho State University, writes about his own experience:

> We undertook an extensive process to devise a reorganization plan. Four faculty committees held 57 meetings, eight of them public forums, to investigate proposed changes. We began with three primary goals: to reorganize units in such a way as to increase efficiency and streamline operations; to enable our institution to emerge from a period of fiscal challenge academically stronger, not weaker; and, if possible, to realize a financial savings that could be applied to the state's substantial and continuing budget cuts for higher education.[40]

This comprehensive, faculty-driven process was exceptionally fruitful and yielded broad results. Olson continues, "not only did we reorganize academic units, but we downsized areas in student affairs and consolidated academic student-support units under a single umbrella, the newly formed Student Success Center, which should allow us to improve student retention."[41]

In these two cases, the difference may have also been in the style of leadership. As we previously discussed, change agents and strategic visionaries both seek similar institution-shifting outcomes. However, they approach it in dramatically different ways. The change agent imposes his or her will on the process, often stacking the deck or short-circuiting deliberations. While these methods may prove expedient, they may also prove disastrous when it comes to ultimate success. The deliberate and inclusive methods utilized by the strategic visionary are designed to create ownership and responsibility. They are slower and often more arduous, but they tend to lead to a successful conclusion.

In December 2008, at the height of the financial panic, the University of Mary hired James Shea, a thirty-three-year old Catholic priest and high school religion teacher, as their next president.[42] The Catholic school in Bismarck, North Dakota, had struggled for years and was now facing the Great Recession. Yet, Shea was optimistic about the future of the institution and began a process that would largely remake it for the twenty-first century. This process would result in Vision 2030, a long-term strategy and audacious $272 million capital campaign.[43] "After two years of consulting and engaging our founding Sisters, alumni, faculty, administration, community members, students, parents, donors, and trustees, we feel this is a collective vision for our future that is robust," remarked Shea, at the press conference announcing the plans in 2015.[44] This deliberate and inclusive strategic visioning process was critical to the institution-altering success that he had in mind. By 2019, they had raised over $100 million and significantly grown enrollment.[45] They had also moved to a year-round calendar, with three trimesters, which allowed students studying at a normal pace to complete a bachelor's degree in three years. The third trimester greatly benefited from the temperate summer weather in North Dakota. Many institutions (Purdue University is a notable example) have spent decades studying and debating year-round calendars, but few have actually implemented one.[46] The process must be inclusive and fair, but it also must drive to conclusion. That is the primary role and responsibility of the leader.

The leadership also has a vital role to play in creating and nurturing a campus climate of collegiality, communication, and transparency. Successful examples of real innovation are invariably found at colleges and universities where the president, provost, and board chair are all devoted to maintaining a healthy campus culture. This is definitely an area where leadership is done by example. Constituents want to see an administration that walks the walk. They also value leadership that can take criticism without taking it personally. Campuses are literally filled with individuals who are trained to question and analyze ideas. That is, in fact, the life of a scholar. Presidents who embrace this reality will be starting in a significantly stronger position than those who do not, and they will be able to build momentum even in very difficult circumstances. Pacing is equally important when it comes to management and operations. Certain ideas and issues will take longer to address and move forward. Again, this is where a president and provost with a strong sense of campus sentiment will inevitably do better. The key is to recognize that there are a range of problems, from mundane to fundamental, that must be overcome through shared governance, not despite it.

The immense financial stresses caused by the Great Recession and the COVID-19 pandemic are central to the third great inflection point of American higher education. The financial realities are stark. Students and families are struggling more than ever with affordability, while institutions simultaneously struggle with deficits. This creates a market dynamic that may make it impossible for either the student or the institution to succeed. The magnitude of this challenge is shaking the foundation of almost every college and university, both public and private. Since these inflection points have fallen fifty to eighty years apart, none of these institutions have the benefit of leadership with experience dealing with such systemic, existential problems. None of them has governing structures that have experience with such difficult times. None of them even has any institutional memory, beyond the historical record, of what it was like to grapple with these problems. Nevertheless, institutional responses to the Long Depression and the Great Depression show us that capable leaders do emerge. They do find a way forward for the institution and its mission, even if the solutions are "radical" or "unprecedented" in the status quo life of the institution.

As we have discussed, successful presidents and provosts achieve these goals by putting the right management and operational structures in place. They make deliberate choices that weigh the many factors specific to an institution, the economic climate, the demographic realities, and so on. This process has certainly become more complicated and will likely remain that way for the foreseeable future. Institutional leaders will probably have to make more frequent adjustments and changes to both management and operations. They will have to remain flexible and able to respond to a rapidly changing landscape. They will also have to utilize governing structures that are not used to dealing with or responding to such rapid changes.

In this vein, they will have to challenge trustees and faculty, alike, to be more nimble, available, and timely. This does not impinge upon or undermine their authority as governors; it simply recognizes their responsibilities when dealing with such challenging times. At Lyon College, the author (King) worked with the board chair, Perry Wilson, to reduce the size of the board and increase the number of board meetings per year.[47] "We truly decided that if we were going to turn the school around, we needed to have a board that was going to be nimble enough to act as quickly as it needed to and board members that were well versed in all aspects of the college," Wilson said.[48] Faculty governance can be similarly restructured to be both more informed, especially at the institutional level, and more timely. For example, many institutions have a budgeting committee that includes significant faculty representation along with the president, provost, and chief financial officer. This committee has great potential for understanding and guiding an institution's financial decisions, rather than being a "rubber stamp" for the annual budgeting process. This will require substantial transparency, a greater commitment to understanding and discussing financial processes and market-driven forces, and probably more meetings. While neither faculty nor trustees will likely relish more meetings, the reality is that shared governance depends on the willingness of the governors to devote time and energy to the process. This is even truer when the college or university is in distress.

As Thomas Paine so eloquently wrote, "These are the times that try men's souls."[49] They are also the times when leaders are made and tested. The greatest test of management is its effectiveness—continuously improved and optimized—despite the circumstances. That is the leadership challenge of management and operations. It is also the promise of the same, since it directly impacts progress and success. No president can be effective without accepting that premise and managing, as well as leading.

4

Stakeholder Relations

In every college there are different levels of stakeholder. The board of trustees and the faculty are the two most powerful stakeholders, bearing their shared governance responsibilities in tandem. Together they form the governance team; however, they function in radically different ways, which makes them a mystery to each other. They represent competing interests with different responsibilities, hold a different sense of timing and a level of historic tension that can alternatively be healthy or disruptive. In this chapter, we examine these differences and recommend strategies for how presidents can avoid animosity and increase coherence and communication between the two bodies. We discuss how presidents, provosts, and board chairs form relationships, alliances, partnerships, and understandings with key internal constituencies. Each utilizes different strategies, based on the peculiarities of the position, which often makes it difficult for leaders to move successfully from one position to the other.

The success of the governance team depends upon two interlocking issues: whether or not team members are educated about the level and limits of their responsibilities, and how well they do their job.

Overall, however, there are very few opportunities to learn the roles related to governance. Faculty leaders rise from among the ranks of their colleagues and may have some level of management responsibility before they take a leadership role, but they typically have little business experience.[1] Board chairs bring the strengths and prejudices of outside work into the job and may have a range of internal committee work to draw upon, but they are often selected before they have a full understanding of how college governance works and the central role—including its limitations—that they play.[2] Perhaps the biggest injustice, however, is that the president's training is often incomplete and sketchy at best.[3] Boards hire presidents for many different reasons, but there may be a problem discovered after the fact. As noted in chapter 1, the search firm and the on-campus visit can help presidential candidates determine if what the search committee says about campus culture is accurate.

If the governance stakeholders can gel and govern as a team, there must be enough interconnected education for them to share a common understanding of campus needs. There are, of course, many programs offered to train senior leadership, whether provided through graduate programs or the national higher education associations. Further, many search firms now provide continued counseling for new presidents, at least through the first year.[4] But there is nothing like an ongoing professional continuing education program comparable to what is possible in fields like law, dentistry, medicine, and nursing. The problem worsens given the difference among responsibilities in the senior administration. It is especially troublesome for presidents who do not have training in the full range of issues they face in their jobs. There are good mentors available, but most presidents and senior staff stumble upon them, ever sensitive to the politics of what happens when you admit that you are unprepared for every challenge.[5]

This leads to the fundamental question of how senior management exercises leadership, while carefully considering stakeholders, from the search process onward. The best presidents know who they are, including demonstrating a comfortable assessment of their own strengths and limitations. There is some level of cognitive dissonance between being genuine and playing the role of president, but stakeholders can spot a phony, schmoozer, missionary, autocrat, usurper, or any of the other countless variations that will define the reputation that a senior leader earns on campus. In public searches, planted questions can test candidates and impair their ability to move forward if their view runs counter to the prevailing interpretation of the correct response on a college campus. Presidential candidates must prepare for the "gotcha" moment during their interviews. Further, members of the search committee can leak their reviews of what they perceived happened in the search. As word leaks out, some members of the campus communities will contact their friends and colleagues on the candidate's home campus to learn more about the candidate, no matter how inappropriate these actions may be. The best trait to maintain through the search is a carefully honed sense of humor.[6]

New presidents work with key stakeholders, especially the board of trustees and the provost, from the moment they set foot on a campus, and they must prepare for the unexpected. Boards often help presidents, for example, by relying on trusted internal staff to prepare for the new administration, but two problems often emerge: first, the board may not understand the inner workings of its campus, relying on perception and internal advice on how best to roll out the new administrator. Second, the campus interpreters may not understand what they are asked to do since they have no training on transition and seldom rely on the experiences of other campuses to help them better understand their role. If the campus interpreter of the transition is a poor communicator or sees his or her role for more than it was meant to be, there can be disastrous consequences for new leadership. New presidents cannot fix a reputation that others constructed for them before they arrive, one that is part impression, part innuendo, and part interpretation.[7]

This is where experience counts, since presidential predecessors may have left critical decisions unmade to preserve flexibility in the transition process, or because it was simply easier to do so in the last months of their tenure. In short, the circumstances that presidents inherit matter.[8] There are always long-term issues to grapple with, including preparing for accreditors, creating a strategic vision, and long-term staffing changes, among many others. Some experienced presidents, like Jake Schrum, who served as president at Texas Wesleyan, Southwestern, and Emory & Henry, believe that good search committees should institute scenario role-playing to determine even before the selection is made if candidates are up to these types of task.[9] Regardless, new presidents should evaluate their capacity to keep their eyes on the forest when presented with decisions that keep them wandering among the trees. Strategic visionary presidents know that good strategy always trumps enforceable tactics. This starts with determining what the issues are and what specific skills can be brought to bear on them. Do you focus inward to respond to internal campus dynamics? Or does the campus need to move beyond the college gates to play a more prominent role in the community? Tuition-driven colleges with large numbers of Pell Grant recipients and high levels of state and federal grants and loans presume that presidents serve as state and national advocates for student aid. Research universities often look more to maintain and increase the research dollars that flow to them. Bad community relations, which include open challenges to the tax-exempt status of the institution, mandate a different commitment of time.

Presidents serve as the pivot upon which all stakeholder relationships are balanced, prioritized, and maintained. As stated, the two most important and powerful college stakeholders are the trustees and the faculty. However, at any given moment, other stakeholders may be equally—or more—important or powerful. Alumni, current students, parents, townspeople, and political leaders may rise and ebb in importance depending on the circumstance. Given the complexity of stakeholders, the ability of presidents to listen is perhaps the most critical first tool to employ. That's why so many presidents begin their tenure by undertaking a listening tour. The tour permits a new president to capture a sense of the place and determine where the sensitivities or minefields lie. These early assessments also permit newly elected presidents to shape their agenda and efficiently craft their calendar. Listening tours better prepare presidents for the balancing act that will be necessary to respond to stakeholder's aspirations and concerns and also helps them form critical impressions of the broader campus community—keys to strategic visioning. Upon settling into her position as president of University of Rochester in the summer of 2019, for example, Sarah C. Mangelsdorf embarked on a "listening and learning tour" on campus and across the country, as do so many of her colleagues, to hear from alumni and other interested groups.[10]

Yet a listening tour, while critical, cannot be the only early accomplishment in the job. The president must lead, and depending upon circumstances, form a team. This mandates that presidents work with the board chair, trustees, provost, faculty, and senior staff if they hope to govern effectively. Presidents must invest their personality, working to develop close relationships with key leaders, creating an especially close understanding with the board chair. These relationships require mutual honesty, transparency, keeping egos checked at the door, and a unified communications strategy to an institution's stakeholders. This extends to key staff, especially the working relationship between the president and the CFO. The success or failure of a presidency can be taken out of the incumbent's hands if the CFO is an institutionalist, ambitious, or inept. Presidents must always remember that, when learning on the job, the best advice is to assume they know little about what they've inherited, no matter how hard they have studied for the new position. Likewise, presidents must always remember: your colleagues either work for you or you work for them.

Presidencies carry perks that allow the holder to use time efficiently, focus on the right tasks, and be rewarded for good work. But in the end, presidents are not autocrats, and there is a difference between friendly professional relationships and deep personal friendships. As noted earlier, the two must not be confused, especially should something go wrong.[11] To offset this range of foreseeable predicaments, presidents should review their human resources practices and protocol. As one president once advised the authors, the first act upon presidential succession should be that vice presidents be required to submit a resignation letter. Although this letter is to be set aside by the president, the act effectively creates expectations around performance, sets a professional tone, and establishes a hierarchy that can make the president's role in governance easier.

Of course, presidents also work for others within the governance chain, and the day-to-day maintenance of stakeholder relationships is a critical part of the job. Presidents should respect their role within governance, not assuming that they are at the top of the pyramid or jockeying for the top position at all costs. Presidents work for their boards. There can be disastrous moments, especially if presidents inherit weak or dysfunctional boards, or chairs who see themselves, to use one example, as business leaders without understanding how higher education works. At the other extreme, presidents who court their boards, or more narrowly, the chair and executive committee of the board, risk an imbalance in their relationship with other stakeholders. One of the worst possible scenarios is when large-gift transactional donors bully boards and sweep over their efforts to manage an institution with their expectations and demands. In one notable example, Lee M. Bass, the Texas financier, mandated that Yale implement a Western civilization curriculum and wanted approval over faculty appointments in return for a $20-million gift in 1991.[12]

Another important role for the president is to serve as the translator among the stakeholders, continually and consistently explaining one body to the other. Each group affiliates with the college on the basis of different experiences, perceptions, and expectations. There is also a healthy tension among stakeholders, especially among faculty, administrators, and trustees. The level of education on the complexity of college operations and the interest that stakeholders have in areas that take them beyond their comfort zones can vary widely. Presidents must serve as "first explainers," working not only to provide education that increases a common understanding but also to tamp down the healthy skepticism that stakeholders have for one another and the president. Early on, presidents must become the voice of authority, using data, facts, a common language, and common sense to explain and interpret what stakeholders say.

Presidents also serve as "first responders" during acute situations, which may run the gamut from a pandemic to community justice issues. It is critical for the president to be the final judge and jury on making the assessment of the situation. Let's assume that a campus-wide issue emerges that has a financial implication and requires a president to act on it. The most seasoned trustees typically take the long view because their duties force them toward oversight. Faculty members are often more cerebral and process driven. Students may feel a need to express immediate emotion about the issue, and their parents want the issue resolved immediately, regardless of the impact on the budget. Yet there are other factors to consider. The CFO rations the budget and may take a very different view of how funds should be spent to achieve a successful resolution. Marketing and communication colleagues worry about the optics on an issue, while advancement officers fret over alumni and major donor reactions. In short, there are a thousand ways to go when a campus-wide issue erupts. The task of the president is to find the common ground, interpret and explain college policy, work with the CFO to find funding when necessary, and nuance whatever optics might emerge. The president may not be responsible for the issue, but he or she must ultimately find a way to resolve it.[13]

Colleges and universities are the collective repository of American culture and much of its evolving intellectual property. As such, they must deal with the immediate moments of crisis—a campus shooting at Virginia Tech or the glaring systemic racism illuminated so tragically by George Floyd's murder and its aftermath in 2020—as well as the lasting implications of the precipitating action. Actions have legitimate reactions that force leadership to lead. There can be impressive statements of early support by leadership, but they must be followed by specific, concrete, and transparent actions to address injustices. A second obvious example is the COVID-19 pandemic. Pandemics can be part of a larger campus planning exercise, but their impact as they worsen can reach everywhere on campus. It is as important to provide medical, psychological, and wellness services on campus as it is to stem revenue losses. The two concerns are not mutually exclusive, and colleges must move past old playbooks to develop a plan for crises, integrate it into strategy, demonstrate their commitment to transparency, and offer identifiable metrics to measure improvement.

That's part of the complexity of the job, especially in an age of immediate social media feedback. Many senior administrators complain that their social media presence bears little resemblance to them. It is a phenomenon shared with the rise of Facebook, Twitter, Instagram, and other social media sites. But the impact on presidents in particular is to diminish the stature of the job. There is no single solution to bad information except to suggest that presidents need to find a middle ground between ignoring "what's out there" and obsessing over it. Presidents must think very carefully about how to craft their own social media profiles. Whatever they do, they should construct a presence that has credibility and transparency and becomes a venue for putting forward facts in support of the college's position. It is always possible to explain a work in progress. Presidents may choose for legal, cultural, or political reasons to say nothing. But they must always be fully informed and tell the truth when they speak.[14] One important rule in public moments: say only what you mean, in as few words as possible.

Beyond an acute crisis, presidents must keep the college in a steady state, especially if they are change agents or strategists. To do so, they must work hard on putting the right effort into stakeholder relationships, but they must set their schedule or risk being pulled in too many directions. This can be difficult, particularly if there are well-established cultural norms that dictate a president's time on campus. The amount of time devoted to a particular topic is a mixture of these norms, personality, the ability to say no to colleagues, and a president's capacity to act not in the moment but in concert with the institution's vision for the future. Donors often give because they have a connection with the president. Presidents should not assume that there is a compelling case for support; powers of persuasion or stellar personality cannot drive a donor to a commitment critical to the institution after a single visit.[15]

Words matter. One of the least attractive aspects of the job is that the words of a president are parsed out, with subsequent interpretation from colleagues and stakeholders, further confusing what a president might have said. But the lesson is inescapable. Presidents are not acting as members of the faculty, nor do they have the luxury of saying the first thing that comes into their mind. They must choose their words carefully, because these words have meaning that perhaps goes beyond their intent among some groups. A president is the principal spokesperson for the institution among the stakeholders, an important public face. Presidents must accept limitations on how they facilitate and interpret their message. It is not a question of becoming someone else. Instead, it is more that understanding the job requires accepting its limitations. To this end, it is sometimes better to be precise and measured than quick-witted and clever, even when demonstrating a good sense of humor.

In the end, the job of the president is about vision, and there is a wide range of opinion on how vision is best expressed. Presidents usually present their vision through a strategic plan, best linked to a campus facilities plan, a solid financial forecast, a sense of what is financially possible, accreditor's reviews, strategic alternative studies, and a branding and assessment exercise that locks in this vision. Some presidents and provosts reject the notion of a strategic plan because they believe that local circumstances determine a vision annually rather than over the uncertainties of the long term.[16] We believe, however, that a visioning exercise is a way of grouping together the stakeholders' hopes and aspirations with the president's own sense of what can be accomplished. In this sense, vision is the glue that makes momentum real for those who have a stake in the future of the institution. While there can be many ways of expressing what's ahead, presidents must offer a clear-headed understanding of what's possible, realistic, manageable, and aspirational.

There are dangers to envisioning the future, however. New presidents often confuse their enthusiasm, ability to sell, intellectual prowess, and creativity with the realities of the boots on the ground. An early and fatal mistake is to promise more than can be reasonably delivered. There are few places in America, for example, that are likely to become the "next Harvard." In the interview and opening statements after selection, presidents must be careful not to lay out expectations likely to bite them as the harsh realities of managing a new campus set in. Further, too much vision early on suggests that presidents may be unwilling to listen to stakeholders, who also have a vested role in shaping it. That said, an institution without a president working to provide vision is likely to tread water in a highly competitive environment.

As we noted earlier, the provost represents the faculty to the stakeholders, including the president. In shared governance, provosts play a bridge role, explaining and interpreting across the campus with language more commonly understood and accepted by the faculty. To do so, they must maintain a separate presence from the president, effectively creating their own space to protect their credibility and ability to advocate without prejudice or personal agenda. The job also mandates a level of loyalty to the president that must be uniform and consistent in practice and policy. It is critical that the provost, in particular, understand this relationship, and that the provost understand the job of the president. Lack of understanding is one reason that many presidents change out the provost within the first couple of years of their tenure.[17]

Yet the role of the provost is also to lead, hopefully in coordination with the president. In the absence of the president from campus, the provost is the immediate court of last resort on matters of policy and day-to-day operations. The provost must have sufficient gravitas and should maintain the same level of professionalism with other members of the senior staff and faculty that the president exhibits. He or she must not exacerbate senior staff territorialism, intrigue, and pettiness. For those provosts emerging from the faculty, one sign of a successful tenure is purely internal, and provosts must recognize that they have moved from faculty to administration.[18] In the best circumstances, senior faculty leadership can guide a provost in protocol and behavior. Provosts must also have good working relationships with their CFOs. Together, they implement the priorities, design and monitor the budget, ration resources, and fund creativity. If the working relationship between these senior administrators is weak or tense, the spillover effect on the cabinet can be enormous. It will further require undue amounts of attention from the president and undermine working relationships among the senior staff and with the faculty and trustees. Taken together, the president, provost, and CFO are the foundation upon which college leadership executes vision. Their relationship requires constant care, a clear definition of individual responsibilities, and a level of trust and respect that often develops only over time.[19]

Provosts must also maintain healthy professional relationships with trustees, with whom they may have had almost no interaction. Trustees may see the provost as a way to influence academic affairs, gather information outside of the proper channels beyond the president's office, or build additional relationships through the senior staff. These actions are inappropriate, but can be governed by wise interactions on behalf of the provost, since trustees have the least experience. The best advice for provosts is to maintain good working relationships with trustees while keeping a respectful distance from them. Trustees are not friends of the senior staff or of the president; they are the governors of the institution. On the other hand, provosts can sometimes see their relationships with trustees as a clear way to grease their succession to the presidency if a change in administration occurs. This approach seldom ends well. In fact, it can blow up badly if the transition is not smooth and if the provost is implicated in the decision to make a change of president.

Two additional duties of provosts determine their success as campus leaders. The first is the ability to give bad news to the president. Presidents live in a cocoon through which they receive highly filtered information, which is often as much what staff think a president wants to hear as what a president needs to know. A provost's relationship with faculty and staff is an extraordinary source of unfiltered information for any president. Good provosts make certain to keep the information passed along unfiltered, but great provosts have the capacity to interpret without a personal agenda.[20] The second duty of provost is almost sacrosanct. Their job is to protect and support the continued, vital role of the faculty in shared governance. Provosts lead the faculty in many ways, some obvious and some more nuanced. Their most valuable role may well be to serve as the interpreters of the faculty to other key stakeholder groups, to ensure that faculty aspirations and needs are understood and appreciated across the campus. They must be certain to guarantee the faculty a role at the governance table and be steadfast in their advocacy, but always mindful that their support of the faculty must be grounded in reality and common sense.[21] They must also work with key faculty leadership to educate faculty and administrative staff about general policy and specific issues that affect the academic program.

Provosts also typically take the lead on the accreditation report. The accreditation report is a clear definition of a campus's "sense of self." It is typically done in collaboration with a task force organized to assist in information gathering, an analysis of the sense of the college, and increasingly, an assessment protocol to determine institutional progress. Provosts must collaborate closely with members of the senior staff, offices, and groups across campus to pull an accreditation report together and form the accreditation committee to research and write the report. This pattern also reflects a similar approach to discipline-based accreditation, which may also be part of the provost's duties. For many provosts, a successful accreditation is the hallmark of their tenure.

It is wrong to assume that holding the job of provost is the equivalent of a minor league tryout for the big-league job of president. Historically, many provosts took this route, but increasingly, provosts are rejecting the opportunity to move into a president's role. Several recent studies show that provosts do not necessarily aspire or transition to presidencies. The 2013–14 American Council on Education's Chief Academic Officer survey noted that only 19 percent of the provosts surveyed became presidents.[22] A 2010 study from the Council of Independent Colleges found, for example, that less than 25 percent of sitting provosts at small- and mid-sized private colleges aspire to be presidents. Survey participants cited a variety of reasons, including the unappealing nature of presidents' work, the negative implications of "living in a fishbowl," the time demands that would be placed upon them, and the fact that many are nearing retirement.[23] It is interesting to note that the average tenure for provosts is only 4.3 years, about half the typical tenure of presidents in 2010, suggesting that presidents may emerge from other areas than the pool of available provosts.[24]

Of the three key stakeholders, the board chair is the only outsider on a college campus. Board chairs are, however, responsible for three key issues. First, they manage the process to select, retain, and replace the president. Second, they shape the discussions that define the program of offerings at a college or university. They do not run the academic programs, but they help set general operational and program policy. The provost and faculty determine the day-to-day operations of the academic enterprise, working with the president to manage it. Finally, board chairs govern by working with their boards to control the purse strings. If an institution runs into financial difficulty by failing to understand and acknowledge what its financial numbers and constraints are, then it is time to replace the board chair. A clean audit does not mean that a college is operating responsibly given the fiscal realities that it faces, especially in the pandemic and the current recession. Higher education is not a for-profit concern. Learn the business of higher education. Then, watch and follow the money to be certain that the institution's house is in order.

As chairs begin their tenure, there must be a clear understanding of what the role means within the board of trustees. Board chairs are not super trustees or cardinals among bishops; rather, their primary job is to lead the trustees. This can involve persuasion, with particular attention to the internal processes of the board. Their job is to manage board relations, draw careful parameters around acceptable board behavior, improve board process and protocol, and keep the board's focus on the potential existential threats that exist on both sides of the college gates. Trustees are the stakeholders who rule on overall strategy, budget, and the administrative team, and the board chair shapes the agenda, timing, and assessment protocol of the board. The chairs' role goes beyond stakeholder to include manager, emcee, and confidant to the president. They create the climate for the success of the administration by using their time, especially in executive session with other board members, to advocate for the administrative team, address private concerns about administration and general direction, and solicit trustee input. In doing so, the best board chairs set the groundwork for momentum on a college campus. This requires maturity, gravitas, and exceptional diplomatic skills.

Chairs hire, support, evaluate, fire, and retire presidents. This responsibility colors the relationship with the president in both positive and negative ways. Most important, perhaps, is that the evaluation responsibility of the board chair carries with it an implied pecking order and prevents most presidents from assuming too much power. One of the first leadership lessons learned by most presidents is to set parameters on how their performance is measured. It is absolutely essential that there be an annual performance evaluation, with rules agreed to and understood by both the chair and the board. One of the clearest signs of potential discord is if a new chair suddenly changes the goal posts on presidential evaluations, bringing in whatever fashionable business practices support the new rules. Beware especially of board chairs with hidden agendas. Sometimes the relationship can be too close, often initiated by presidents as a way to insulate and protect their jobs. Whatever the approach, the relationship between the two should be cordial, professional, and a priority for both of them. Friendship emerges and often grows deeper as both individuals come to understand the difficulty and appreciate the synergy of their work together. When selecting a chair from among the trustees, nominating committees deciding on a new board chair must think carefully about fit with the president. They should vet their prospective board chair carefully. Otherwise, the outcome can create a governance crisis with scars that can take years to heal.

The board chair also has an important ceremonial and set of delineated roles to play beyond presidential evaluations. In matters that cut across campus decision-making and at times of institutional crisis, the board chair is often the primary voice of the institution. This first responder role comes into play when dealing with personal tragedy or loss, presidential wrongdoing and succession, and major institutional direction, including the announcement of a capital campaign, realignment of mission, or during groundbreaking facilities ceremonies. The trick is to know when to take center stage. Good chairs first consider whether it is a policy or an administrative issue. If it is administrative in nature, the principle should be to let the administrators do their job without interference from the board chair.

The board chair has a day-by-day operations role that is critical to good governance. The chair must coordinate the interest and actions of the trustees who are the least experienced and knowledgeable about college governance. On any board there is a considerable amount of bickering, individuals who jockey for position, and bad board fits among the trustees. In general, most boards are far too large and inefficiently run.[25] A good number of them are highly politicized, and some operate as extensions of the institution's alumni network. Good chairs begin by assessing how best to professionalize the board. This requires considerable stamina, patience, humor, and a steady hand, particularly when the management of trustees challenges established processes. Keep this always in mind: the chair runs the board that governs the institution. Bad, uninformed boards, overwhelmed by process disguised as institutional tradition, can spell disaster for a college or university. It is necessary, therefore, to build a board that is policy focused. The best board chairs understand that the institution they serve cannot exist in a vacuum and that colleges have important local, state, regional, and national relationships. They exist in a hypercompetitive business environment where the largely unregulated actions of peers and aspirants can have an immediate and deleterious impact upon their bottom line, especially at tuition-driven institutions. Chairs must choose the three to five areas in which their leadership matters most and which best support the president and faculty. They must create a climate where trustees can learn the craft of higher education, recognizing that it is often more an art than a science. With this responsibility comes the need to create transparency across governing groups and with key constituencies, including the Faculty Senate, Alumni Board, Parents Board, and other groups. Communication must be clear, regularly conveyed across several venues, and prioritized by levels of importance.

Finally, board chairs, like presidents, must know when to leave. That decision should be framed by the board's policy on succession. Occasionally, presidents, other board members, or influential donors might attempt to weigh in on the tenure of the chair, and so it is important to have a rigorous annual board evaluation, regular retreats that include time to review governance policies and protocols, and the board's feedback on the chair's management. There should be well-established and broadly communicated policies in place for the selection process, length of term, its limited renewability, and the process of succession. Chairs must prepare for their departure from the moment that they take office. In a process-driven campus culture, there should be smooth, uninterrupted governance to be certain that the governors have unimpeachable credibility with all stakeholders.[26]

Beyond shared governance, no groups other than trustees, senior administration, and the faculty have responsibility for the governance of their institution. There are other groups of stakeholders, however, who influence the discussion. Each has its own way of fitting into the decision-making process, with the approach varying widely across higher education. These "influencers" include but are not limited to students, staff, alumni, parent boards, and major donors, as well as various advisory councils to the provost and dean in areas such as academic disciplines and student life, and athletic and other affinity groups, including Greek life, where applicable. The mix is different at every institution. But the governance stakeholders ignore them at their own risk. Students are the focus of the institution. Beyond them, parents often have their fingers on the pulse of the campus. They want immediate change to benefit the limited time span of their children's attendance.[27] Alumni often best remember the institution that they left rather than think more strategically about where the college or university is headed.[28] And donors, especially the ones who see philanthropy as though it were simply a transaction, can be especially bothersome.

It is essential for the board chair and the president to have a plan in place to deal with these groups, one that includes setting limits, incorporating good ideas, and placing time constraints on their own outreach toward these groups. The dangers are obvious. Students and alumni in the days of social media wield a loud voice, which has a public dimension that can impede progress and redefine efforts at transparency in negative ways, no matter how noble the effort by the stakeholders to communicate. Helicopter parents may advocate for their children, effectively diminishing the need for students to emerge as more independent and ready to enter the workforce. Among the most notorious transactional donors, money may talk too loudly, sometimes creating awkward and even impossible choices for the other stakeholders, especially a president with a weak board. The trick is to balance the authority granted by the charter, mission, practice, and protocol with the politics of inclusion among stakeholders and related groups of influencers. Sometimes it works, but on other occasions the road can be bumpy and the solution imperfect.

Collectively, these groups of stakeholders coexist within the business of higher education. For most presidents reflecting on their stakeholder groups, it is best to think of their leadership in political terms. Being president is a bit like being a strong mayor in an environment that operates like a New England town meeting. Everyone has a vote or assumes they do. Presidents need to listen to their constituents, build consensus, settle on a policy, and tie the history of the institution to where it is and where it must head to remain sustainable. But there is one other function that is essential. America's colleges and universities can no longer exist as isolated "cities upon a hill." They are academic enterprises. But they are also economic engines for their towns, regions, states, and in many cases, nationally or even globally. How they shape their environments beyond the college gates has deep implications for their vitality, the optics that emerge, and their ability to remain relevant.

5

Campus and Community

S takeholders extend beyond the faculty and trustees. They include
students, staff, alumni, parents, friends, and community support-
ers. What leadership role does a college or university play in these
communities? How should its strategy reflect its role? A college campus can be a closed, inward-looking space operating at times like a
kind of haven from the unpleasantries of the outside world. Our mission is to create an academic enterprise that flourishes because of the
knowledge of its professors, the skill of its staff, the curiosity of its
students, and the quality of its programs.

The facts support an additional purpose. The size and stability of
colleges and universities in a community shape the future of their local
environment. A college is a substantial neighborhood, local, regional,
national, or global enterprise, depending on its purpose, reputation,
scale, and mission. The judicious use of people, programs, and facilities
improves a community, enhances the climate, and effectively grows
the college or university as an economic engine to improve its region.
In this chapter, we describe a spectrum, from a small college's effect
on a rural town to a major "eds and meds" teaching and research in-

frastructure's effect on a region, while examining the underlying dynamics that can lead to success or failure. The academy has an outsize effect, due to its dual role in the creation and transfer of knowledge. That is its unusual role to play in the community and the world.

While colleges and universities do not run as for-profit enterprises, they contribute as much and often more to their region than other employers because they invest heavily in people, land, and facilities, thus tying their future inexorably to their hometowns. They have a dominant economic, social, political, and cultural presence in a community. While some may argue that taxing college lands would better support the local tax base, colleges stabilize and improve communities by making them more desirable places to live and creating a public good for which they earn a tax exemption.[1] It's ultimately a quality-of-life question for the citizens who live in college towns. Because colleges don't manufacture products or sell services, their benefits can be hard to see, touch, and feel, even though they contribute human capital to the workforce.

Colleges also maintain expansive, largely well-tended physical plants, especially if they are residential colleges or create large research facilities. For the uninitiated observer, these institutions often resemble spas, with significant over-the-top investments in student service facilities, such as theaters, dining complexes, and athletic venues.[2] They look and often act as if isolated and standing apart from their neighborhoods, separated by a wall, real or imagined. While a college degree may be a ticket into the middle class, the physical appearance of many colleges suggests a perceived elitism that exacerbates town-gown relations. Local public perception can miscast a college as an isolated, arrogant, unfriendly "city on a hill," removed from their surroundings by preference and choice. College leadership can contribute to this perception.

Colleges and universities are easy targets in their communities. This is especially true in cash-strapped towns with a deteriorating tax base. But the criticism leveled by detractors can also be as much about what they represent to a community. Students live on campus and in the surrounding neighborhoods, but they may make vastly different use of time than their neighbors who complain of late-night parties, trash, noise, and a failure to respect property.[3] Colleges and universities bring into a community commercial services that appeal to students but may seem detrimental to the rest of the town. Yet students also bring vitality and contribute enormously to their host communities. There are innumerable examples of volunteerism at social service agencies, volunteer rescue and fire departments, EMT services, and neighborhood clean-up efforts, for example, to counter the claims brought against students. And that's the problem. A college community is a living, breathing, dynamic extension of a town, warts and all. The result is a constant give and take, with the governing stakeholders on both sides typically on the receiving end of the problems that arise.

Why, then, should presidents, board chairs, and other stakeholders pay attention to their community? While colleges and universities must do a better job of asserting their value as academic institutions, they must work even harder to establish their role as economic engines that contribute human capital to the workforce. The income disparity that exists in those areas of America that are booming—New York, Boston, Washington, Pittsburgh, Minneapolis, Austin, Atlanta, San Francisco, and Los Angeles, to name a few—emerges in part because "eds and meds" and their spin-offs have created it.[4] The impact in rural areas may be even larger. What would upstate New York, western Pennsylvania, and the rural upper Midwest look like if the economic engines powered by public and private rural campuses closed? State and federal politicians would be wise to think about the devastating impact on their regional economies before they push free public tuition and free community college programs, potentially forcing a number of private colleges out of business.[5]

There are dozens of examples that we might provide to make this point.[6] To illustrate, we looked at the impact the closing of St. Joseph's College had on the town of Rensselaer, Indiana. At the moment of closure, then president Robert Pastoor noted that the 128-year-old institution would need $100 million to remain open, with an immediate infusion of $20 million before the end of their fiscal year. He asserted that, "despite our best efforts, we were not able to escape the financial challenges that many tuition-dependent smaller universities have faced in the past several years."[7] Mr. Pastoor noted that high levels of debt, fear that the college would permanently lose its accreditation, pressure from auditors that would limit access to student loans, and depreciated, deteriorating facilities had forced the closure. Its accreditor, the Higher Learning Commission, had placed the college on probation through 2018, identifying concerns over "resources, planning and institutional effectiveness."[8] While detractors may fault process and transparency as conditions deteriorated, St. Joseph's College was an anchor and major employer in its region. Its closure offers a lesson on how economic engines can flame out, often quietly and without much fanfare, but the community impact can be profound.

In the case of St. Joseph's, the college employed more than two hundred individuals, making it a major employer in a town of six thousand people in a largely agricultural region. The city of Rensselaer also took in significant income from the campus's utilities use, which totaled $640,000 in 2017, according to Rensselaer's mayor. Local businesses were concerned about the ripple effect that the loss of nine hundred students would have on the region's economy. As Melissa Shultz, a local businesswoman and lifelong resident lamented to the *Chicago Tribune*: "I just don't want this to become a ghost town."[9] In many ways, the loss to a community like Rensselaer is comparable to an auto plant shutdown or a mine closure, but with an important distinction. The business of higher education is a public good, established to prepare educated citizens for the workforce. Colleges bring visitors to Main Street America, anchor the cultural, social, and economic quality of local life, and provide continuous stable employment in a way that a manufacturing plant cannot. The lesson of St. Joseph's should serve as a warning shot across America about what happens when bedrock institutions that define entire towns disappear.

All of the campus stakeholders have a role in managing a higher education institution's relationship with its neighborhood. The board must be supportive of any engagement for at least two reasons. The first is that such an engagement will likely come with a financial cost to the institution, no matter how successful a college or university may be in using combined state, federal, and private resources. The second is that any engagement will require leadership, beginning at the top, with the president. The faculty's role is also important, especially in supporting town-based academic program engagements and student service initiatives that enhance social and cultural life. In addition, many senior staff and faculty also serve on the boards of local non-profits, banks, religious institutions, social service agencies, and related groups and businesses.[10] But the president, together with assigned members of the senior staff, is the principal architect of a town-gown strategy that will determine how the relationship unfolds.[11] Boards will need to understand that the involvement of presidents in their region is expected and necessary because academic programs create economic engines that sustain their regions.

For presidents, the first question is always how much time should be devoted to local social and cultural commitments, regional activities, and state and federal service. The best advice is to look situationally at where the college or university is in the community, what opportunities and challenges exist, and how they can best work to improve their community. What's best going forward? Beyond the obvious hope that relations get better over time, new presidents should always understand as much about the communities in which they live as possible. They should also ration their time carefully, depending upon where the institutions' strategic vision will take the institution. A combination of subjective and objective research must be employed. The investment by an institution's leadership is critical, however, with local, regional, state, and federal officials watching carefully to determine how well presidents listen to them. One lesson is that it's important to listen before you lead, with an understanding that these first interactions can shape how presidents are perceived throughout their tenure. It's ultimately a test of presidents' diplomatic skills.

Washington & Jefferson College provides an interesting case study. As cash-strapped municipalities in Pennsylvania openly agitated for payment-in-lieu-of-taxes (PILOT) programs to offset their revenue declines, the situation came to a boil in Washington, then a small, declining industrial city about thirty-five miles southwest of Pittsburgh. The

City of Washington filed suit against Washington & Jefferson College, a small, highly selective liberal arts college noted for educating many of Pittsburgh's doctors and lawyers, by challenging its tax-exempt status. The suit made it all the way to the Pennsylvania Supreme Court, which ruled in favor of the college. The national higher education associations joined in an *amicus* brief to support Washington & Jefferson. Most of Pennsylvania's private colleges and universities, which saw the handwriting on the wall, contributed to a fund to offset the cost of Washington & Jefferson's legal battles. The Pennsylvania Supreme Court's decision remains a defining legal ruling in the United States, even today, in support of the continuing tax-exempt status of nonprofit organizations, including colleges and universities.[12]

As the new president, elected just months after the Pennsylvania's Supreme Court's 1997 ruling in favor of the college, the author (Mitchell) was tasked with picking up the pieces after a battle that had left local community leadership with a bitter aftertaste. He immediately opened a dialogue with city officials and county commissioners. In their meeting with him, the commissioners unloaded on the new president with a litany of wrongs that went back more than fifty years—not entirely unexpected, given the contentious court battle. After the meetings, Mitchell argued that the college's new strategic plan would shape tactics that could bring both groups together. The first marker was pledging that Washington & Jefferson would no longer be seen as uninterested in the city that surrounded it.[13]

To fulfill that pledge, Washington & Jefferson sought and received a grant from the Benedum Foundation to organize a meeting to bring townspeople, politicians, business leaders, and college officials together over several months to develop a framework for engagement. One of the first outcomes was an improvement in the tone and tenor of subsequent discussions and rising levels of civility, despite the heated passions expressed by participants. As the conversation continued, participants increasingly recognized that the college should be defined by what was reasonable and fair to meet unanswered community concerns. The college agreed that it could do more to support the police and fire departments, commercial interests in the downtown, and the social and cultural life of the city. Perhaps most important, however, was an effort to chart a common set of priorities based on the recognition that each group contributed in ways that were strategically important to the other. For Washington & Jefferson, these meetings served to refine the college's reputation as a contributor to the neighborhood, and more generally, to Pittsburgh and southwestern Pennsylvania.[14]

The Washington & Jefferson experience illustrates why towns must matter to college leadership. The best answer may be the most obvious one. We live there. Richard Florida's terminology—"the creative class"—looks to town-gown relations that are open, supportive, dynamic, and vibrant, effectively nurturing a quality of life that makes communities more attractive for the residents and the students, faculty, and staff who work at an institution.[15] But there is also a practical concern. Admissions officers at well-respected institutions are sometimes careful, for example, to steer incoming students away from adjacent neighborhoods for fear of how it could impact on their first-year yield.[16] Revitalization efforts, like those pioneered in Philadelphia, by the University of Pennsylvania and more recently by Drexel University, demonstrate the importance of safety, access, and convenience blended into curbside appeal.[17] The danger of students summarizing their college experience as "I loved the school but hated the town" will have deleterious impacts on the college's financial bottom line, public image, and ability to maintain lifelong relationships with its "influencer" alumni base.[18]

A key financial concern is the ever-present challenge by local authorities to the tax-exempt status of a college or university. Colleges and universities must make every effort to quantify and publicize their contributions locally, regionally, and statewide. Dynamic and growing towns whose leadership understands a college's contributions to its community may still have community leaders who grouse about specific issues, but they are less inclined to attack an institution using legal weapons or through political posturing. They are often more open to nuance, looking at innovative partnerships that produce common investment strategies, many of which are designed to increase the tax base. Local politicians share the desire to protect their quality of life, which is also in the interests of the college. This is one area in which faculty and staff can use the community—their neighborhoods—to create teachable moments outside classrooms and labs.[19]

The best strategic thinkers in higher education recognize that any visioning at a college or university should account for the broader environment beyond the gates. Perception matters. College leadership must shape and control perception by ensuring that a college strategic vision is also a statement on why their surroundings matter. If visual perception begins with curbside appeal, colleges have no choice but to invest in their towns and work with the economic and political leadership to shape their common environment. A dynamic environment also attracts investors—including students, families, faculty, staff, alumni, donors, and friends. In the twenty-first century, colleges and universities also invest in their communities because it offers them a competitive advantage. In the end, those institutions with the best relationships, clearest town-gown synergies, and broadest community dialogue create the best-defined identity. You know it when you feel it on a college campus, and an attractive physical space in a growing and dynamic city or town improves yield.

Even before a college or university concurs on the need to invest in its environment, the president must make some early decisions driven largely by history and mission. How does the institution see itself in the world? Thomas Jefferson designed the University of Virginia, for example, as an "academical village," built on "the most extensive and liberal scale that our circumstances would call for and our faculties meet," drawing students from "other states to come, and drink of the cup of knowledge."[20] The great public universities founded after passage of the Morrill Land-Grant Act in 1863 sought to create institutions "without excluding other scientific and classical studies and including military tactics, to teach such branches of learning as are related to agriculture and the mechanic arts, in such manner as the legislatures of the States may respectively prescribe, in order to promote the liberal and practical education of the industrial classes in the several pursuits and professions in life."[21] This differentiation in purpose and program created a decentralized American higher education system of public and private colleges and universities, but it also profoundly affected the role that each institution played in its community.

In approaching community relations, one must understand mission and circumstance. Colleges and universities constantly evolve as living and dynamic institutions, but they have a history that blends the "academical" with the economic. Presidents must decide, therefore, what their definition of community is before they can determine how much time they will allot to nurture it. The economic and structural health of a community can identify immediate and mid-term needs that must be met to maintain peace in the neighborhood, the vitality of a downtown, and the economic strength of a region. But history and mission also shape town-gown relations. In every case in which the authors have been involved in community relations, the response to nurturing and strengthening a sense of community was different. Williams does not respond as the University of New Mexico does, nor should its leadership expect to do so. Not all institutions face as bitter and divisive a challenge to their tax-exempt status as Washington & Jefferson did in the 1990s. But the test of leadership for presidents and those working in external and government relations is to appreciate that they don't get to choose how to work through the problems that are unique to their institution.

Circumstances shape leadership, often in unforeseen and unexpected ways. Most presidents devote some time looking beyond their municipal boundaries to better reflect the history and role they must play in the region and beyond to support the mission of their institutions. This requires that they participate in state and federal lobbying, cultural, social, and economic associations, and academic groups.[22] Colleges and universities cannot live in a vacuum, as the range of their influence always extends beyond their neighborhoods. In a sense, working to build a broader community is also an act of self-preservation. While these institutions are by and large tuition-driven, they rely on state and federal loans and grants to pay the bills and public support to make their case as a public good. In 2017, for example, the US government contributed $78 billion to postsecondary education, and higher education was the third-largest area of general fund spending at the

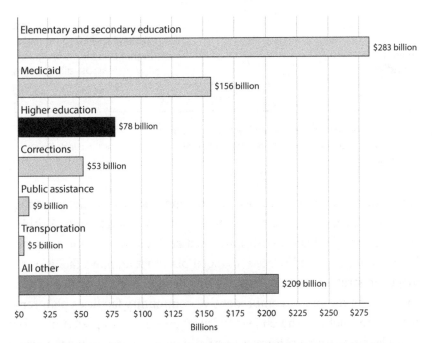

Figure 5.1 bar chart data:

- Elementary and secondary education — $283 billion
- Medicaid — $156 billion
- Higher education — $78 billion
- Corrections — $53 billion
- Public assistance — $9 billion
- Transportation — $5 billion
- All other — $209 billion

(x-axis: Billions, $0 to $275 in increments of $25)

Figure 5.1 Major categories of state general fund spending. "Two Decades of Change in Federal and State Higher Education Funding," *Pew Charitable Trusts*, Oct. 15, 2019, https:// www.pewtrusts.org/en/research-and-analysis/issue-briefs/2019/10/two-decades-of-change -in-federal-and-state-higher-education-funding.

state level, behind K-12 education and Medicaid (see figs. 5.1 and 5.2).[23] How colleges and universities spend their tuition dollars will also be affected by their tax-exempt status, the state and federal regulatory climate, and the stewardship of local politicians. As higher education continues to evolve, it seems increasingly inevitable that regional accrediting agencies will focus on how academics and economics intersect, looking beyond the strength of an institution's balance sheet to determine how successful a college has been as an integrated and helpful citizen, with senior leadership serving as advocates for the communities and constituencies that they serve.

That said, higher education leadership lives in a world shaped by the aftermath of the Great Recession a decade ago, the current steep economic downturn, and the COVID-19 pandemic. If we accept the argument that America's colleges are bedrock institutions in their

2%
Federal spending on major
higher education programs
across all agencies

Figure 5.2 Comparison of state and federal spending on higher education. "Two Decades of Change in Federal and State Higher Education Funding," *Pew Charitable Trusts*, Oct. 15, 2019.

community, officials must become far more skilled at determining what resources they have to use in community engagements. Within this context, the best institutions must seek constant improvement, linked to a vision and related financial plan that employs facilities to meet the strategic plan's goals set within their broader contribution to their community. A comprehensive community facilities plan represents and defines the college culture, presents an opportunity for first-glance curb appeal for prospective applicants, and provides a powerful, visual statement of institutional confidence and determination to be an active participant in the growth and well-being of its community. It is also a significant indication of differentiation among peer and aspirant institutions. Thriving college cities and towns simply sell better to prospective students, faculty, and staff. They seem safer, especially to worried parents. Colleges seem more vibrant and dynamic places when they fit seamlessly into their surroundings.

To be effective, the college's stakeholders must think differently about how their construction program is put together. They must start by determining whether the existing town is already an asset to the college. Is the commercial core sufficiently near the campus to matter? Are the college's existing town-gown policies, including cash and in-kind support where offered, sufficient to promote transparency in communication and a common purpose? The way town-gown relations play out is different in each circumstance, but college administrators must shape their involvement to meet the criterion that it fully invests psychologically, culturally, socially, and economically in its region. Each college must engage the community with a clear head, shaped by a basic understanding that colleges and communities need each other to prosper and survive.

At least three factors shape this thinking: strategy, purpose, and control. The best strategic plans look at the full range of college assets. Presidents should seek a strategic plan that links the college and its environment. These plans see connections between ambition, need, and opportunity. Can campus space be freed up by transferring college assets—museums, student housing, theaters, sports venues, business incubators, and administrative operations—into a town? Can a college or university simultaneously use its resources to shape campus boundaries? It begins when college stakeholders, most notably reluctant boards of trustees who shape overall college policy, look at how their environment can become part of its asset base.[24]

Purpose is the toughest nut to crack. In post-recessionary America, how should colleges use their precious debt capacity? Does it make sense to use bonds, fundraising proceeds, and operational surpluses to finance new construction beyond capital expenses in an annual budget? Or, alternatively, are there certain combinations of programs and facilities that lend themselves to third-party financing and development, freeing these sources for other uses, including funding depreciation and supporting endowment growth?[25] For example, student services administrators, working with a college's accountants and lawyers, may be able to connect facilities to academic and student service programs within residence halls. Student services programs imply a social contract between students and their institutions. If the social contract determines their relationship, is it necessary in every case to control the building in which the social contract is executed? In circumstances in which off-campus student housing predominates, is it possible to improve the recommended range of housing off-campus without incurring additional upfront student costs? Can a college blend this housing into a more vibrant revenue- and tax-producing campus edge or downtown, which positively influences campus appeal in admissions?[26]

The issue of control ultimately becomes a test of leadership. It's always easiest to abandon cooperative partnerships in favor of institutional control; indeed, campus inertia encourages little change in established practices concerning how people and programs intersect with the campus master facilities plan. The status quo defines the chain of command in ways already acceptable to the campus community. It's easier and involves less paperwork for senior staff, who are often uncomfortable working in areas where they have limited expertise. Facilities directors are often overly concerned about private developers' abilities to meet an institution's standards for construction, while CFO's and college counsel argue that tax-exempt bonds are critical to cost-effective building projects. The sense that "we've never done it this way before" often drives these arguments.[27] Higher education leadership, looking across the full range of assets and sensitive to finding new ways to finance college operations, must be prepared to respond. Reserving bond capacity for academic programs is often a compelling argument to support change in financing approaches.

There are very real hazards to cooperative partnerships, especially with some of the innovative public-private opportunities that exist. Not long ago, most senior college administrators—and the boards who took their leads from them—had little tolerance for private investment, using debt, fundraising, and surpluses to meet their facilities' needs.[28] They made a good case. These administrators argued that they could use their existing debt capacity, with historically low interest rates, their ability to fund deferred maintenance, and their need to control design, construction, and outfitting to ensure a well-run college or university.[29] The first realignment occurred when public college administrators began to reexamine this argument, looking to third-party developers to house students beyond the college gates. In larger settings, this effort to meet internal housing goals incorporated even greater changes, which impacted the commercial district that surrounded them. This blend of commercial and residential construction spread to other institutions.[30] Arizona State University's redevelopment of their Tempe neighborhood is an outstanding example of constructive use of public-private partnerships.[31]

College administrators, led by the presidents and their boards, can use public-private partnerships to meet strategic needs that link real estate, student services, academic programs, facilities expansion, and town/gown relations together in new and innovative ways. This approach has spread to a good number of small private colleges as a tactic to upgrade their facilities, meet new student housing needs, and encourage higher enrollments.[32] Or, it may be a test run at "strong balance sheet" institutions like Middlebury.[33] Other public institutions, such as California's community colleges, are also imagining residential construction to house students as their own mission evolves and becomes more complex.[34] The need to continuously improve a campus has created massive additional institutional debt, edging many colleges to the end of their debt capacity.[35] Boards recognize the problem, but many need to concentrate more intensely on how debt is used as part of their general oversight responsibilities. Depending on location and mission, it's quite legitimate for presidents, boards, and faculty leadership to ask if a college operating a residential student life program needs to be in the hotel business to do it.

Leadership involves choices. Whatever the decision, the risks are clear, depending on where you sit. Senior college administrators must keep a watchful eye on competitive consumer demands, their own strategic direction, and whether the revenue from student housing and related ventures is necessary. Whatever steps are taken, higher education leaders must also recognize that they lack in-house experience to complete significant, complex public-private ventures. They must look beyond their expertise to see where best practices and prudent advice exist across higher education institutions and their providers. If the redefinition of the tuition financing model is at hand for higher education, then it's time for colleges and universities to look at underutilized assets like real estate, tax credits, state economic development partnerships, and federal programs for colleges like the USDA rural development initiative to fund and sustain their future.[36] College administrators, faculty, and their boards must always remember that they oversee an institution more akin at times to a small town than a for-profit corporation. In doing so, they must stage the implementation of their strategy as a kind of multidimensional chess game, being certain to make sure they use all the pieces on the board.

Large or small, the underlying dynamics of how colleges operate in their communities is similar. The way their leadership approaches the creation and transfer of knowledge is different, shaped by scale and mission. But the impact of a college on its community is outsized when compared to that of other large employers. The stakeholder leadership must always know where they are in addressing community relations. Indeed, many new presidents drawn into leadership positions from diverse environments are shocked by the complexities they face in town-gown relations and the social and cultural requirements that are necessary to maintain them. For some presidents, membership in the Rotary is expected; for others, it's a misuse of precious time. Diplomatic skills are important because the college's stakeholders often set the tone of a community's agenda. It's essential that the leadership of any higher education institution be keenly aware of their surroundings. Knowing when to listen, when to speak, and learning how to draw the line on the use of rationed college resources sets the foundation for subsequent community discussion. In the end, the college's leadership, led by the president as the administrative head of the institution, represents the college in public settings. Community relations is a twenty-four-hour job, shaped by optics, community opinion, and social and print media.

The specific approach and subsequent ramifications differ in every instance, but the impact of colleges on their regions can be enormous. There must be synergy between the college and the community. Austin would be a moderate-sized state capital without the impact the University of Texas and its spin-offs have had on the region. Boston can lay claim as the "eds and meds" capital of America, thanks largely to the impetus from spin-offs created by MIT and backed by enlightened state policies that directly supported biotechnology and the life sciences.[37] The San Francisco Bay area's economic strength draws directly from its foundations in the region, led by anchors like the Stanford Technology Park and the growing technology and commercial base in Emeryville, near the University of California at Berkeley.[38] Rice University donated the land for the Johnson Space Center and organized world-class space science programs.[39] North Carolina's Research

Triangle Park, linking the University of North Carolina, Duke, and North Carolina State University, among others, changed the economic development parameters in North Carolina forever.[40] In almost every state, America's colleges and universities have contributed a disproportionate share of the knowledge transfer necessary to support this growth.

When dealing with the community, presidents and other higher education leaders must appreciate both the academic enterprise and the economic engine that supports it. Together, they create the rationale for a broader conceptualization of a college community, closer to the original Greek definition of the academy. In ancient Greece, the academic enterprise fostered and promoted a cultural accumulation of knowledge, transmitted across generations by its practitioners. The underpinnings of the Greek academy had similar expressions across the ancient world, in China, India, Persia, Africa, and elsewhere.[41] American colleges and universities remain the beating heart of America, and indeed, of global cultural transmission. They are the repositories of our collective knowledge. But they also transfer that knowledge and, in doing so, create their own synergies to affect how their environments evolve. They cannot survive in isolation. Colleges and universities are in the business of higher education. Higher education is among America's leading industries, educating millions and employing a large skilled workforce that keeps our cultural transmission alive. Putting the campus into the community requires a delicate balancing act, which campus stakeholders at each institution must think through carefully to get right.

6

Accreditors, Athletic Conferences, and Beyond

In this chapter, we further examine how those on the outside impact the way in which senior stakeholders exercise leadership, both by narrowing the constraints through which leadership is exercised and by placing institutional leadership in a broader context than what happens locally on a college campus. Put in other terms, good leadership places an institution within a decentralized system of higher education nationally and globally, building relationships that merge internal standards, practices, and beliefs with the challenges and opportunities that are driven by regulation, market, and consumer tolerances. How senior leaders demonstrate leadership off campus will greatly influence the path forward for the institutions they serve.

The breadth of outside organizations and affiliations differs from institution to institution. However, most institutions are associated with a regional accreditor, an athletic association, and an athletic conference. Most are also members of national and state associations. The work of these associations ranges from government relations and advocacy to shared member services and collaborations. There were

878 colleges and universities with religious affiliations in 2017.[1] These institutions relate to their associated churches in a variety of ways, ranging from covenants and episcopal representation to freestanding organizations, such as the Association of Presbyterian Colleges and Universities, the National Association of Schools and Colleges of the United Methodist Church, and the Association of Catholic Colleges and Universities. Leadership in this ecosystem of organizations is a complicated matter of balancing the needs and prerogatives of the individual college or university with its commitment and duty to serve the larger community of peer institutions. This is a challenge that vexes many presidents and provosts, but it is a challenge that must be met for the long-term success of the institution.

According to the Council for Higher Education Accreditation, "Regional accrediting commissions are among the oldest accrediting organizations in the country. The United States is divided into six accreditation regions: New England, Middle States, North Central, Southern, Western, and Northwest. Seven accrediting commissions operate in these regions. All regional accrediting commissions review entire institutions, as opposed to programs or schools within institutions."[2] The Serviceman's Readjustment Act of 1944, or the G.I. Bill, created the need for large-scale accreditation following World War II. Returning veterans were provided with the largest federal student aid in US history.[3] Millions availed themselves of this support, pushing institutions to capacity and beyond. This influx created a unique problem when it came to graduate and professional education. Abbott writes, "for those men and women who lived in states which sponsored no public schools of medicine, dentistry, veterinary medicine, and other professional disciplines, it was becoming increasingly difficult to gain admission to the professional schools of states that did."[4] In 1948, the Southern Regional Education Board was conceived at the Southern Governor's Conference to address this and other issues associated with collaboration between and the quality of education and degrees across institutions of higher learning in different states. In short order, each geographic region began a similar effort, and the six regional accreditors coalesced. Ultimately, the federal government would rely predominantly on these regional accreditors rather than develop a national body.

This regionalism creates a unique challenge for leaders, especially if their careers take them from one accreditor to another. In general, the principles of accreditation and philosophy of self-regulation are similar across the seven regional commissions. "The empowerment flowing from self-regulation promotes both innovation and accountability in achieving the goals of educating and training citizens in a representative democracy . . . accreditation is best accomplished through a voluntary association of educational institutions. Both a process and a product, accreditation relies on integrity; thoughtful and principled professional judgment; rigorous application of requirements; and a context of trust," states the Principles of Accreditation of the Southern Association of Colleges and Schools Commission on Colleges.[5] As you can see, peer relationships play heavily in the process of accreditation. The reaffirmation process, in which every institution is routinely assessed to maintain its accreditation, is primarily driven by a committee of volunteers from peer institutions. In fact, the final stage of reaffirmation involves an extensive multiday site visit from this committee. History and relationships among these visitors and campus leadership can heavily influence trust. If the campus leadership is new to the region, these relationships simply may not exist, and the process may be more difficult.

Beyond peer relationships, the evolution of the regional commissions has led to differences in their processes. Some accreditors stick to a rigid ten-year periodic reaffirmation. Others have more flexible processes, which are left to the individual institution to choose. For example, the Higher Learning Commission pioneered the Academic Quality Improvement Plan in the 1990s. This "pathway" was set on a shorter, eight-year cycle, with more routine interim reporting.[6] The goal was to help institutions achieve continuous quality improvement, in addition to the regular quality assurance and institutional improvement.[7] While the AQIP pathway is currently being phased out, it shows how different the process can be from one region to another. Presidents and provosts who are new to a particular accreditor should be diligent in their approach to learning the nuances. They should also be deliberate and active in building relationships with the new commission and its member colleges and universities. This includes attending the annual meeting, volunteering to serve on a review committee, and serving on the governing board and committees of the particular accreditor.

While regional accreditors dominate the landscape for institutional accreditation, national accreditors lead the way in accrediting particular programs or schools. For example, by a federal statutory mandate, the Council and the Accreditation Committee of the American Bar Association Section of Legal Education and Admissions to the Bar are recognized by the US Department of Education as the accrediting bodies for programs that lead to the JD degree.[8] The process is somewhat similar to that of regional commissions, using peer-review committees. However, the periodicity is every seven years. In 2011, the *Chronicle of Higher Education* reported that the Association of Specialized and Professional Accreditors had sixty-one members, up from forty-six a decade earlier.[9] Today, the ASPA has members ranging from the National Architectural Accrediting Board and the Accreditation Board for Engineering and Technology to the National Association of Schools of Dance and the National Association of Schools of Art and Design.

As the number of specialized national accreditors has grown over the decades, so have their requirements. "They blackmail us," said John V. Lombardi, the president of the University of Florida, one of the few top university leaders willing to discuss the issue openly. "If they say your department of astrophysics needs 12 spaceships and you have only 10, you had better get the other two," Mr. Lombardi added wryly, "You take the money from the history department because it doesn't have an accrediting lobby to protect it," reported the *New York Times* in 1998.[10] Unlike the regional accreditors, national accreditors are far more likely to judge programs based on resource allocation, such as square footage of facilities, type, availability, and age of specialized equipment, number and expertise of faculty members, etc.

"If you don't go along with their demands," Lombardi said, "they can deny accreditation in whatever it is that they represent, and then, even if they don't control Federal loans and grants, they can tell the state legislature that you lost your accreditation and the legislature will fire all of the top people who run the institution."[11] While these are hyperbolic observations, they illustrate the real delicacy of dealing with accreditors, especially for specialized professional programs. These programs carry little or no tuition discounting, based in part on the affirmation of and association with a "name brand" accreditor. Therefore, they are often critical to the financial health of the institution.

While part of the job of a president or provost is to represent their institution to the accreditor, the other part of the job is to work on behalf of the accreditor as an active participant in insuring the quality, continuous improvement, and financial health of peer institutions. This is especially important in times of great stress on colleges and universities. In the summer of 2020, the commission announced that, "in light of the financial and operational pressures caused by COVID-19, the Higher Learning Commission is shifting the Financial Indicator process to a more time-sensitive model in 2020. HLC is requesting information from member institutions whose recent Composite Financial Index score fell to [a greater level of concern]. HLC has developed a short survey that the Chief Financial Officer will be asked to complete on July 1, September 1 and November 2."[12] Early in the pandemic, the Middle States Commission on Higher Education announced that it would "temporarily waive the substantive change requirements for distance education for institutions not approved to offer this alternative delivery method."[13] The rapid and comprehensive response of accreditors was driven by the self-regulating community of higher education leaders who make up the ranks of their governing boards and senior staff. While accreditors are often portrayed as "the other," come to judge a college or university, it is important to remember that they are us in a very real sense.

Athletic associations and conferences are the other great realm of peer-run, self-regulating organizations in higher education. The National Collegiate Athletic Association (NCAA) and the National Association of Intercollegiate Athletics (NAIA) have a combined member-ship of almost 1,350 colleges and universities in the United States.[14] Intercollegiate athletics in the US began in 1852, when Harvard and Yale met in the first crew rowing competition.[15] College sports are now an important part of the undergraduate and alumni experience at most institutions. Colleges and universities have storied teams, traditions, and rivalries. Even diminutive St. John's College plays the US Naval Academy annually in croquet (the Annapolis Cup). Sports serve as a widely enjoyed activity for students in general and student-athletes in particular. They form the backbone of alumni support and branding. At many colleges and universities, they are the principal con-nection to alumni, often have a direct interrelationship with Greek life, and attract the most outside social media and print press. Never-theless, athletics do not pay for themselves. Stakeholder leadership must think very carefully about their costs and benefits, how much control to exercise, and how much disruption will be tolerated by con-stituencies. Presidents, faculty chairs, and board chairs are often at odds about how to care and feed athletics. The role of athletics must be shaped by campus culture and not by special relationships.

The two associations differ in both scale and approach to scholar-ships athletics. NCAA is by far the larger organization, with almost 1,100 member colleges and universities, divided into three divisions. "Division I schools generally have the biggest student bodies, manage the largest athletics budgets, and offer the most generous number of scholarships," notes the NCAA website.[16] NCAA says its Division II schools "provide thousands of student-athletes the opportunity to compete at a high level of scholarship athletics while excelling in the classroom and fully engaging in the broader campus experience."[17] In addition, "Division III is unique in not awarding athletic scholarships due to its unwavering commitment to the academic success of every student-athlete . . . Division III student-athletes compete not for fi-nancial reward, but quite simply, for the love of the game."[18] NAIA, on the other hand, has a single scholarship division, in which all 250 mem-ber schools participate.

The two major athletic associations are made up of 123 conferences.

These conferences, large and small, share similar governing structures. Each has a commissioner who reports to a council of presidents, representing each member institution. The athletic directors from each college or university form a separate council. The two councils work in consort to both govern the conference and run it season to season. The presidents and athletic directors also attend the annual meeting of the athletic association, where they participate in the larger governance of the division and organization. Because conferences have championships with one another, their governance and operations intermingle. This milieu provides the president with an opportunity to develop collegial relationships with presidents at very different types and sizes of institution. While this is beneficial to the functioning of the athletic association, it is equally beneficial to the president and his or her institution. It creates a cross-pollination of ideas and practices, as well as a fertile ground for potential collaborations and partnerships that go well beyond the athletic realm.

On campus, successful leadership requires thinking about how athletics can be run efficiently, how much debt should go into facilities construction and redesign, and what the scholarship maximums the operating budget will tolerate at Division I and II levels are. This calculus would be relatively straightforward if one had to consider only operating costs, capital investments, and the like. However, intangibles, such as alumni sentiment and brand awareness, may be equally or more important when it comes to athletics. Nevertheless, the leadership should endeavor to model all of these factors and make data-informed decisions accordingly. Presidents should invest an equal amount of diligence and caution in the connection of athletic directors and coaches to trustees and alumni, and occasionally, with faculty and staff. Leaders should be aware of back-channel communications, which shape perceptions about their decisions, style, and the quality of their leadership. Any president who has had to fire a football coach knows the swift wrath that such a decision can visit upon him or her. While that may factor into a president's planning for such a change, the decision should favor the greater good of the institution.

Presidents should also consider the overall burden of athletic programs. With many colleges and universities struggling to break even, it is incumbent upon the leadership to be realistic and thorough in their examination of the costs and benefits of athletics. Based on a ten-year self-study, the NCAA reported that "the expenses generated by operating athletics programs continued to exceed the revenue they produce at the vast majority of Football Bowl Subdivision schools."[19] Kathleen McNeely, NCAA's chief financial officer, stated that there is still a misperception that most schools are generating more money than they spend on college athletics. These data show once again that the truth is just the opposite."[20] In a time when expenses are being scrutinized more than ever, this scrutiny must extend across the entire enterprise. This certainly includes athletics. Otherwise, presidents risk the legitimacy of any efforts to reduce costs and balance budgets and invite warranted criticism that can seriously undermine trust.

Smart leadership makes certain that general wellness, both physical and psychological, factors heavily into student life programs. This suggests that athletes should be integrated into student life rather than be "cocooned" from it. Good leadership mandates active intramurals, health and wellness options, options tied to areas from which recruiters are drawing students, and strong outdoor programs. Presidents must put their foot down and out speak against "Taj Mahal" facilities, which run up debt and exceed the purpose of athletics on campus—the so-called jockplexes. If possible, large-scale facilities should be community based, public-private partnerships, with the college or university exercising the lead. This will not only share the burden of cost, but more importantly, it will greatly increase the potential utility of the facility for the whole community. It may also serve as an important catalyst for conversation and collaboration that ultimately benefits the town-gown relationship, in addition to the project at hand.

Beyond the average campus, collegiate athletics and its role in society can be murky and troubling. It is no secret that scholarship athletics, especially in the "big-time" conferences, is the tail that wags the dog. Will Hobson writes, "The payout rules are complicated but enticing. Even if your college basketball team doesn't win a game, you win $1.67 million. A round-of-16 appearance rakes in almost $5 million. A

Final Four run? $8.3 million. What sounds like the country's most lucrative office pool is actually how the NCAA splits up much of the $700-plus million its men's basketball tournament makes each year."[21] Yet, the scholar-athletes who produce this annual windfall are not compensated beyond the college education that they may or may not complete. The majority of these players are black, from low-income, first-generation college-attending homes. The majority of head coaches are white, with six and seven figure annual salaries.[22] The men's basketball tournament basically funds NCAA's existence, with 40 percent of the proceeds going to support NCAA's annual operating budget.[23] It also funds the operations of many of the conferences. "'The standard of living, if you will, is really dependent on the men's basketball tournament,' said Tom Yeager, commissioner of the Colonial Athletic Association," reports Hobson.[24]

For over a decade, NCAA and its member institutions have also sought to capitalize on the names, images, and likeness of its student-athletes. In 2009, the Ohio State University licensed these to Learfield IMG College for $11 million a year. NCAA followed suit with a similar deal with the video game company Electronic Arts. Other professional athletic associations, such as the National Football League, cut similar deals but also passed on significant portions of the revenue to the players.[25] The inequity is only made starker when viewed through the lens of intellectual property. Imagine two undergraduate students at a large research university. One receives an academic scholarship, while the other receives an athletic scholarship. If the first student were to produce valuable intellectual property in the course of his or her studies or unpaid research, the student would own that property outright. If the second student, through extraordinary athletic performance, were to also produce valuable intellectual property (i.e., their own image and likeness), the student would own nothing.

After ten years and many lawsuits, the NCAA and its members finally yielded to overwhelming public sentiment in regard to this inequity. In 2019, NCAA Board of Governors voted to allow college athletes to profit from their name, image, and likeness. Jemele Hill notes that "if the NCAA is bending slightly to the popular opinion that athletes should be able to cash in, it isn't because the organization suddenly caught a case of common sense. It's because the NCAA didn't have a choice."[26] Lawmakers in several states had begun proposing legislation that would have allowed it, whether or not NCAA did.[27] Recognizing that athletic associations and conferences are peer-governed and self-regulating, they have to get better at leading the way forward on challenging and correcting these inequities. Rather than hunkering down in a defensive posture, they have the ability to be progressive forces.

In the wake of George Floyd's killing by police in 2020, the NCAA and its conferences began to utilize their bully pulpits in a progressive manner. "It was just before 9 a.m. [June 19—Juneteenth] when Philip Gunn, the speaker of the Mississippi House of Representatives, received a phone call from a lobbyist for Mississippi State University. The National Collegiate Athletic Association, the lobbyist said, might soon take a punitive stand against the state flag, the last in the nation with the Confederate battle emblem, just as the Southeastern Conference had done the night before," writes Alan Blinder.[28] Coaches descended on the capital the following week to lobby lawmakers. Only days later, on June 30, the governor signed a law to remove the confederate emblem from the flag.[29] This is the power for good that college athletics can wield if the academic leaders who govern have the fortitude to use it.

National higher education associations, such as the American Council on Education, the American Association of Community Colleges, and the National Association of Independent Colleges and Universities, play a vital role in representing the interests of higher education to the nation. This is where policies on student aid, the regulatory climate, and tax issues are addressed. These organizations are often "president-based," in that they are both governed by the member presidents and also rely on these presidents to do much of the organization's work. College and university presidents must train themselves in these broader issues and be prepared to assume a leadership role, especially in states that have key congressional leadership. They must take the time to really learn the issues, in depth and substance, so that they can be effective advocates. Finally, they must dedicate the time to do this work. That may be the most difficult aspect, since there are so many competing interests for the presidents' time from their own institutions. Nevertheless, this work on behalf of the collective will ultimately benefit their home institutions.

National organizations go beyond advocacy to focus on areas of deep interest across higher education. For example, the Association of American Colleges and Universities' strategic plan addresses substantial challenges: "Among the most urgent challenges facing colleges and universities today are growing economic, racial, and ethnic segregation and an intolerance for difference. Accompanied by a burgeoning loss of public trust, the notion of higher education as a public good has been displaced by a belief that a college education is a private commodity. Calls for a demonstrated return on investment measured solely in terms of employability have intensified."[30] The organization is working with their member presidents and provosts on a variety of initiatives to address these very issues. These include a truth, racial healing, and transformation effort (in partnership with the W. K. Kellogg Foundation), a religious differences initiative, pathways for underserved student success initiative, and an initiative to advocate for liberal education with systematic employer surveys.[31] Working in collaboration, the members of the association can accomplish far more than they could individually. Other national associations, such as the Association of Governing Boards, work to better educate and prepare trustees for their governance role. These organizations, alone and in consort, make their members better institutions and advocate tirelessly on their behalf. They can be of great utility to presidents, provosts, and board chairs if utilized properly.

State associations play the same role as national associations but at the state level. For the wealthier schools, it is both a practical matter and a matter of good citizenship to participate in state associations. For the less well endowed, it is often a question of survival, especially if they are heavily dependent on state and federal aid. Like their national counterparts, these organizations are largely "president-based." The presidents usually form the governing board of the organization.

They are often called upon to serve as advocates with the state legislatures. The history of many of these organizations is tightly bound with the creation of special-purpose legislation to supplement the tuition of students choosing to attend private colleges and universities in the state. For example, the Council of Independent Colleges in Virginia was founded in 1971, with state aid for private education in their mission. According to their website, "CICV is proud to have played an instrumental role in starting the state's Tuition Assistance Grant (TAG) program. TAG provides annual grants to Virginia residents who are full-time students at an eligible private college or university. In 2018–2019, approximately 23,000 Virginia residents will receive non-need-based tuition grants of $3,270 (undergraduate) and $1,640 (graduate students in health professions)."[32] These organizations routinely advocate for the continuance and expansion of these programs. The Independent Colleges and Universities of Texas hosts visits to the capital for its member schools during every legislative session. This includes students visiting the House and the Senate, as well as visiting individual legislators to speak directly to the importance of the tuition equalization grant they receive.[33] This advocacy also extends to the media. State organizations often maintain active media contacts and work with their member institutions to project a unified message and a common agenda.

Some state associations have member service programs, which enhance creativity, create efficiencies and economies of scale, and cooperatively address the regulatory environment. The Association of Independent Colleges and Universities of Pennsylvania maintains a corporate affiliates program that includes discounted pricing and enhanced service for insurance, utilities, student loans, facilities management, cybersecurity, retirement and benefits, professional services, group purchasing, etc. With almost ninety members, these institutions reap the benefits of scale that few could get on their own.[34] As small colleges and universities come under increasing financial stress, state organizations have an important role to play in finding more collaborative efficiencies. These efforts should be supported and promoted by their stakeholders. Ultimately, both national and state associations are the products of the leadership provided by their member presidents. Those that have groups of strong leaders are truly effective.

As we noted earlier, a significant number of private colleges and universities are affiliated in some form with a church or religious organization. Historically, this can be attributed to the westward expansion of the American frontier. Catholic dioceses and orders and Protestant denominations founded colleges soon after they formed churches in a particular region. These colleges would educate their congregant's children and produce clergy in addition to their greater service to the community and region. The nature of the college's connection to the church depends on how the original charter was established. Some have very close corporate connections, while others are much more loosely affiliated. The author's (King) current institution, Lyon College, is a good illustration. It was founded in 1872 in Batesville, Arkansas, by Presbyterian pastor Isaac Long and his congregation. In the aftermath of the Civil War, the region was recovering and desperately needed educational options. The college's modern connection with the church takes the form of a covenant, regularly renewed, with the Synod of the Sun, Presbyterian Church (USA). This covenant includes the college's commitment to "the concerns of the church," such as, "representing the Christian gospel . . . while remaining hospitable to people of other faiths" and "creating an environment in which individuals may develop deeply-held values."[35] The church has an active role in the governance of the institution, namely, the Synod elects trustees presented to it by the board's governance, nominations, and compensation committee. Nevertheless, its control is constrained: "While the Synod may advise or request the Board of Trustees to take or to refrain from taking a particular action, the Synod cannot require or instruct the Board to do so. The relationship between the two bodies is one of mutual trust." The church also makes commitments to the college, such as providing financial assistance and promoting the school within its congregations. While this covenant is illustrative, many institutions have much stronger connection and control.

In late 2019, the South Central Jurisdictional Conference of the United Methodist Church sued Southern Methodist University after the university announced that it was severing its ties with the church.[36] This rupture occurred because the church expanded its prohibitions on the performance of same-sex marriage and the ordination of gay and lesbian clergy. A similar split was occurring within the denomination itself, but that did not stop the church from rapidly asserting its legal authority. The lawsuit states, "SCJC founded SMU in conjunction with an initial gift of 133 acres that, to this day, comprises SMU's main campus in Dallas County, Texas. For more than a century, SMU and its governing documents have acknowledged that SCJC is the electing, controlling, and parental body of SMU."[37] It goes on to allege that "the Trustees of SMU had and have no authority to amend the Articles of Incorporation without the prior approval and authorization of SCJC" and request that the court nullify the November 2019 Articles and void any actions taken in reliance upon those Articles.[38] Finally, it affirms that SMU is "to be forever owned, maintained, and controlled by the South Central Jurisdictional Conference of The United Methodist Church."[39] Clearly, this illustrates the opposite extreme of a university's connection with a church.

Based on the examples above, the leadership challenges for a president or board chair can range from mild church politics to internecine warfare. Nevertheless, the president and board chair have very different leadership roles when it comes to these connections. The board chair may be connected with both the institution and the church; indeed, this may be required. She or he must carefully balance these two relationships, especially if they have governing and fiduciary duties on both sides. Care should be taken to avoid conflicts of interest and to thoroughly document them if they exist. The chair should ensure that similar care be taken by other trustees who may have overlapping responsibilities. Beyond governance, the board chair should work to maintain a healthy productive relationship with the clergy and laity who work on behalf of the church in this mutual relationship. These relationships often transcend presidential leadership, since the average tenure of a president continues to decline.[40] The president, on the other hand, has a primary responsibility to the college or university. Like the board chair, the president has to work to maintain good relationships with the church. However, the president is at all times representing the college or university. The president also acts as the bridge between faculty governance and the church. This can be challenging at times, to say the least. Faculty's primacy over the curriculum can come into conflict with the church. It is up to the president, and the provost to a lesser degree, to manage these conflicts as they arise. Transparency is a necessary tool in this regard because it is the basis of trust, and trust must be maintained if these conflicts are to be overcome. Like dealing with any other organization on behalf of the college, the president's active, engaged leadership is critical to the success of those relationships. The relationship with the church is no different.

Many church-related colleges and universities are also members of an association of church-related peer institutions, like the Lutheran Educational Conference of North America. Similar to other national organizations, these are largely "president-driven" operations with an annual presidents' meeting. However, they may also have meetings for chaplains and even faculty (e.g., Annual Conference of the Association of Lutheran College Faculties).[41] These organizations can be useful for presidents in a variety of ways. First, they provide a group of peers who have extensive experience in working with the particular church. Second, they facilitate a coordinated effort and approach to the church. Third, they provide a smaller venue for discussion among presidential peers who may be dealing with similar institutional issues. Finally, they advocate for higher education within the church as a whole. This may include everything from securing additional financial resources to providing a pipeline for students. In any case, these associations can be very useful to a church-related institution.

A president may also be asked to serve on external boards, both nonprofit and for-profit. Service on local nonprofit boards can provide a stronger connection with the community, entrée to events, access to important individuals or donors, and so on. Service on regional or national nonprofit boards can be equally beneficial. Beyond the benefits to one's institution, it can be important to one's professional development. Service on business and corporate boards puts the experience and wisdom of the academy in corporate board settings. Because colleges and universities are economic engines, understanding corporate America is vital to successful college leadership. The better college stakeholders understand economic development and workforce preparation, the more balanced their judgment will be about the outcomes their institutions must produce. Corporate board participation will also deepen the college and university brand, open key (and often new) professional contacts that benefit the institution, and pave the way into corporate and foundation support available only to stakeholders that maintain high visibility.

In all of these settings, presidents have the opportunity to build relationships that can lead to new opportunities for their college or university. An athletic conference meeting might focus on how sports can be used to build leadership skills—the discussion might even lead to new opportunities for academic collaboration among conference members. These sorts of coalition of the willing are built on relationships and leadership. They project beyond the often myopic and mundane considerations on an isolated campus. They break through calcification, and they have the power to change the conversation. For all these reasons, presidents should be diligent in giving these activities and relationships the dedicated time that they deserve. This may mean challenging trustees, faculty, and even students who want the president to be ever-present on campus. That nineteenth-century conceit is no longer a path to success. True leadership will recognize that reality and take a firm stance on the importance of relationships beyond the college gates.

7

Measuring Success

Success and *failure* are not normally the words that come up when colleges and universities do assessment and institutional research. While success may be hard to measure, failure can be devastatingly simple. The brochure for the auction of Green Mountain College's campus read, "85 Percent Off . . . former campus of Green Mountain College . . . ideally located on the New York border in the Southern Vermont lakes region . . . 22 impressive buildings, housing for 654 students, 33 classrooms, library, indoor pool, 400-seat theater, and a farm with barn and greenhouse . . . Auction date and time: Tuesday, August 18, 2020 at 1:00 pm."[1] The college's 185-year history was reduced to a list of capital assets being sold to pay creditors. Institutional failure is measured in the detritus of what is left when the college or university can no longer fulfill its mission. Thankfully, most institutions never have to endure failure of that magnitude; nevertheless, many are facing challenges greater than they have faced in generations. Presidents and board chairs must be equal to the task and active in their approach to strategic assessment. This is different from the sort of routine assessment conducted under the watchful eyes of accreditors and generally led by the provost. It is more focused on the long-term ability of the college or university to fulfill its mission.

Trustees and faculty play a key role in large-scale strategic assessment. Unfortunately, both groups may have significant deficits to overcome. Trustees are the least tutored and will need to understand how to assess a higher education institution rather than their own businesses, and also learn how to assess themselves. In regard to the first point, many trustees begin their work knowing little more than what it was like to be a college student (decades earlier). Therefore, the orientation process should be comprehensive and thorough. Since enrollment drives revenue, it is important to cover the recruitment and admission process, specifically, yield, tuition discount rate, and room and board auxiliaries. Higher education expenses differ significantly from what many trustees may have encountered in their careers. First and foremost, there are many more fixed costs, and inflation, as measured by the Higher Education Price Index, is substantially higher than for the wider economy, as measured by the Consumer Price Index (CPI). These inputs and outputs are fundamental to understanding the economics of the business of higher education. Governance also differs substantially from what most trustees are used to seeing in corporate governance. Namely, the academy utilizes shared governance split between the trustees and the faculty. Trustees should understand that their role is primarily fiduciary in nature. The only active operational roles they have is approving the annual budget and hiring, reviewing, and terminating the president. Nevertheless, they do play an important role in planning and assessment, starting with themselves. Board assessment is critical to a full spectrum of how trustees educate themselves about their role. The board chair should be evangelical about this and ever diligent in policing trustee overreach into operations.

Faculty are products of the academy, but they often arrive not fully understanding their responsibility in shared governance. The faculty play a critical role in ensuring that the curriculum and academic programs are properly assessed, especially in light of the accreditor's concentration on institutional quality, consistency, and continuous improvement. These concepts were famously pioneered in postwar Japan. Fujio Cho, president of the Toyota Motor Company, summarized: "The key to the Toyota Way and what makes [the company] stand out is not any of the individual elements . . . but what is important is having all the elements together as a system. It must be practiced every day in a very consistent way—not in spurts."[2] This is what the faculty can bring to both institutional assessment and shared governance, namely, a firm commitment to constancy and consistency. Unlike the trustees, the faculty are on the ground every day. This gives them important experience and powerful insights, which they bring to their governance role. Faculty leadership (existing in that nebulous state between faculty and administration) should also be assessed by the faculty with input from the administration. Faculty leadership should have a clear annual agenda and cooperate in assessing institutional goals. Finally, like the trustees, the faculty should put in the time to understand the changing dynamics of enrollment (e.g., demographic shifts), higher education costs, median family wealth and income, etc. This will make them better partners in shared governance.

Beyond their separate governing responsibilities, the two bodies have to work together to understand each other and the challenges that each group faces. This is where the administration, particularly the president and the provost, can play an essential part. The president, who is often simultaneously a trustee and a faculty member, is the glue that bonds the governors together. The provost, who works very closely with the board and its committees, should be a strong partner in this bond. Together, they are often called upon to represent one side (or one side's interest) to the other and vice versa. However, these leaders cannot be the only bridge. A healthy board structure almost always includes appointed faculty representatives. Their official duty may be to express and protect the faculty's interests, but their unofficial duty—getting to know and building collegial relationships with trustees—is equally important. This can help address many of the strong biases and picayune tendencies common to trustees, especially those new to college and university board service. For example, many new trustees question the need for academic freedom and tenure. While the president and provost should be able to give a thoughtful and full-throated argument for both, faculty representatives can serve as a living, working embodiment of why these things matter. That is often more persuasive than even the best reasoned arguments. The shared governors, together with the administration, must build a relationship of mutual respect and trust if they are to accurately measure the success of the institution. This has never mattered more than it does now, in an era when so many colleges and universities are facing existential threats.

In their book *The College Stress Test*, Robert Zemsky, Susan Shaman, and Susan Campbell Baldridge write, "Might it be possible to know now which institutions are most at risk of failing in the future—either closing outright or being absorbed by another, more successful provider? The answer, we decided, was yes, provided there was at hand a means for calibrating the market stresses each institution is likely to face."[3] The College Stress Test they developed examined institutional factors, ranging from market segment and geographic region to average enrollment and financial health. The first factor, market segment, involved developing a taxonomy that objectively placed any given institution within the marketplace. They settled on five categories:

—*Medallion*: the segment comprising the nation's most competitive institutions and students; a segment for which prestige-based ranking plays a substantial role in defining institutional ambitions and quality.
—*Name Brand*: a segment largely populated by well-known institutions. Most practice selective admissions, though their appeal is more likely to be regional than national. Many but not all of these institutions would like to be Medallions.
—*Good Buy*: a segment comprising a variety of institutions, for the most part offering full-scale undergraduate programs at prices substantially less than those of higher-ranked institutions.
—*Good Opportunity*: a segment comprising institutions and students who see higher education as a special opportunity. Many students who shop in this segment are the first in their families to attend college.
—*Convenience*: the one segment in which part-time and intermittent

learners dominate. Students in this segment often shop for a friendly environment at an institution that understands special needs, including the need to take courses at convenient times.[4]

This taxonomy, along with regional demographic shifts, is shown to be highly predictive in regard to enrollment dynamics. Four-year public medallion and name-brand institutions have seen very little in enrollment losses, while four-year public, good buy, good opportunity, and convenience institutions have seen substantial erosion from 2008 to 2016 (figure 7.1). For four-year private not-for-profit colleges and universities, only medallion institutions have been immune from losses during the same time period (figure 7.2).

Regionality has also played significantly into enrollment trends, with the West Coast fairing far better than any other region. As discussed in the introduction, these regional demographic trends are only going to increase in significance during this decade, with large swaths of the country seeing a decline in the college-going population.

Of course, there are many ways to assess a college or a university's financial health. *Forbes* magazine developed a system to grade the fiscal viability of private not-for-profit institutions based on data submitted to the US Department of Education's Integrated Postsecondary Education Data System database. The components of this analysis included endowment assets per full-time equivalent student, liquidity

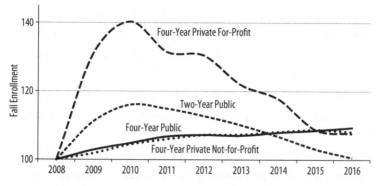

Figure 7.1 Fall enrollment of undergraduate degree-seeking students by sector, 2008–2016. Robert Zemsky, Susan Shaman, and Susan Campbell Baldridge, *The College Stress Test* (Baltimore: Johns Hopkins University Press, 2020), 21.

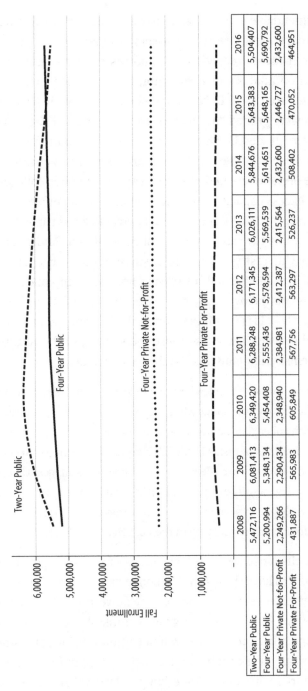

	2008	2009	2010	2011	2012	2013	2014	2015	2016
Two-Year Public	5,472,116	6,081,413	6,349,420	6,288,248	6,171,345	6,026,111	5,844,676	5,643,383	5,504,407
Four-Year Public	5,200,994	5,348,134	5,454,408	5,555,436	5,578,594	5,569,539	5,614,651	5,648,165	5,690,792
Four-Year Private Not-for-Profit	2,249,266	2,290,434	2,348,940	2,384,981	2,412,387	2,415,564	2,432,600	2,446,727	2,432,600
Four-Year Private For-Profit	431,887	565,983	605,849	567,756	563,297	526,237	508,402	470,052	464,951

Figure 7.2 Fall enrollment of undergraduate degree-seeking students by sector, 2008–2016. Actual counts. *Source:* Zemsky, Shaman, and Baldridge, *The College Stress Test*, 22.

of assets, expendable assets relative to debt load, core operating margin, tuition dependency, return on assets, admission yield, percentage of first-year students receiving aid, and instructional expenses per FTE.[5] Based on analysis of these data, they assigned institutions a grade ranging from A+ to D. Not surprisingly, only 34 elite (medallion) institutions were graded A+. Of great concern, over a third of the institutions were graded D. This number rose from 110 in 2013 to 177 in 2019, an increase of 61 percent.[6] Much of this decline is based on the competitive pressure created by excess capacity. "Public colleges have 6.4 percent excess capacity, growing at about half a percentage point a year. But the private colleges have 12.4 percent excess capacity, growing at about triple the rate of public colleges," Kevin Coyne, a professor at Emory University's Goizueta Business School, says. "Here's the worst news. The smaller half of private not-for-profit colleges, those with enrollments below 1,125, have overcapacity of 28 percent and growing rapidly."[7] It is incumbent upon the leaders and governors of colleges and universities to use these tools and take the results very seriously. Zemsky, Shaman, and Baldridge conclude:

> Whatever the pressures on leaders to publicly spread their school's good news, what do we know about what they are thinking privately and discussing with colleagues behind closed doors? As one indication, let's look at the findings of *Inside Higher Ed*'s annual anonymous survey of college and university presidents in 2019. The results suggest that many presidents are generally aware of the risks to the industry at large, and some—"nearly one in seven"—are worried that their own school may be at risk for closing or merging in the next five years.[8]

The great challenge for presidents and board chairs is getting trustees and faculty to have these difficult conversations. The level of denial can be extreme. Never underestimate the powerful effect of nostalgia on the ways in which these two groups think about the institution. Trustees harken back to the days when tuition was low, and students could realistically work their way through college in four years. This avoids the stark reality of the underlying inflation that drives the cost of higher education and associated increases in tuition. It also ignores the corrosive effects of increasing tuition discount rates in a race to the bottom to attract students in a contracting demographic. Whether it be the 1950s, 1960s, or the 1990s, many trustees remember a time of great expansion in higher education. These decades were also periods of great economic growth, which resulted in federal budget surpluses.[9] Alas, times have changed.

Faculty often exhibit similar tendencies. Many senior faculty members began their careers in the 1990s and fondly remember double-digit endowment growth year after year. They also remember the free-spending ways associated with that largesse. Their nostalgia is for the institution that existed when they arrived. The same goes for enrollment and academic profile. Faculty members remember the steady year-on-year increases in the early 2000s, forgetting the precipitous downturn in prospective students resulting from the Great Recession.[10] As colleges and universities struggle to make a class, they have often had to compromise selectivity and academic profile. This can be a serious point of concern and irritation for the faculty, who remember the rising selectivity and academic profile of students earlier in their careers. They may see it as some nefarious scheme rather than as driven by the market realities of declining numbers of college-going students and shifting regional demographics. Again, times have changed.

Presidents and board chairs should be creative in their use of planning and routine governing processes to drive necessary conversations among trustees. Any strategic planning can be front-loaded with copious amounts of anti-nostalgia, state-of-the-institution data, market analysis, demographics, historical budget and financial analysis, etc. Ideally, this will not be simply handed out, but presented in a compelling interactive way by internal and external experts. Alternately, routine processes, such as the annual audit, can be much more informed and informative. A good auditor ought to have a portfolio of similar higher education clients, which can serve as useful anonymous peer comparisons. Many trustees may be surprised to find that the college's financial struggles are shared by many other similar institutions. These sorts of peer comparison also allow for discussion of strategy.

For example, if most or all of the peer institutions are relying on a growth strategy to balance the budget, growth is unlikely to be a competitive strategy for most, if not all, of them. Just knowing that can bring a board new insight.

Presidents and provosts should work together to do the same with the faculty. They can use existing committees, processes, and programs to provide much more information and context. Traditional assessment surrounding reaffirmation by a regional or national accreditor can be approached in a more global manner, with greater emphasis on peer comparison. This can include everything from their student learning outcomes to changing student populations. Are our peer institutions adapting more quickly and effectively? Budget and planning committees can be given interactive presentations similar to those provided to the board regarding the changing landscape of higher education. These same committees can be challenged to reassess peer and aspirant institutions, picking colleges and universities that are much more realistic and useful as comparisons. Faculty governing processes can be more generative, moving beyond an exploration and analysis of the current environment into the future of their institution's place in the emerging environment. Finally, new venues and conversations can be facilitated that let the faculty, trustees, staff, alumni, and other constituencies explore these things together. Success is not going to happen in a vacuum, and the more engaged the constituencies, the more likely new strategic directions and options will succeed.

The real challenges come when measuring success shows signs of significant or existential failure. Trustees and faculty may go from nostalgia and complacency to overreaction, micromanagement, and panic in short order. As more and more colleges and universities come to the precipice of failure, either through outright closure, eliminations of colleges and schools, or clumsy mergers and acquisitions, leadership is going to be especially strained. University and college boards should ask whether they have the right leadership to weather this third inflection point. Does their current leadership have the right mix of strategy, operational knowledge, and financial expertise to shepherd the college or university through this crisis? If the answer is no (or their president has recently resigned or retired), they should be taking immediate action to secure the leadership that can save them. This means employing a search process that does not drag on for almost a year, which is closer to the norm than the exception in higher education. While this elongated process might be defended in a more normal economic environment, it seems reckless and dangerous in the current situation. As the crisis deepens, trustees should recognize that their fiduciary responsibilities require them to question and take responsibility for how presidential searches are conducted. Given the crisis, the selection should be based on the cold, hard facts about the level of stress that exists, along with an understanding of how the candidate must demonstrate strategy and vision to adapt to the new global environment buffeting American higher education.

As discussed previously, we believe that presidents tend to exhibit three distinct leadership styles. In more normal times, this may not matter as much. Search committees tend to rely more on "fit," a vague and debatable notion of how any particular candidate might engage with the community and perform on campus. Certainly, the chosen candidate must believe in and embody the mission. However, this is different from leadership style. During a crisis, there may be nothing more important than leadership style. It is hard to imagine a presider doing well in this environment. At best, he or she will be especially thorough in examining the strategic options. This might be acceptable if the board chair has a more aggressive style, but it risks the chair feeling the need to get involved with operations. At a critical time, this overreach might cause further instability. A change agent or strategic visionary is much more likely to be effective, but their approaches will likely be very different. In true bull-in-a-china-shop fashion, the change agent may feel the need for immediacy. This "emergency response" might yield results, but it might also undermine shared governance, diminish transparency, and lead to other problems. Alternately, the strategic visionary will likely balance the need for expediency with the need to choose the right strategic option. She or he will not undermine shared governance but will insist upon an expedited process. This will likely lead to a better strategic response, one that is borne out in the short and the long run.

With the right leadership in place, the process of examining options can begin. While this process may vary widely depending on the particular situation, it will likely have many common elements. First, there will be an institutional recognition that a significant problem or set of problems exists. These will probably be recognized through the normal assessment processes, although the details may be confidential. Second, the trustees and faculty will be called upon to weigh in on the situation, not with solutions per se but definitely with thoughts and opinions. Third, a variety of options or potential options will be developed. This process may involve the entire shared governance structure, or in the case of more sensitive matters, a representative but limited group. Fourth, an exploration of these options will commence, whose purpose is to determine the viability and impact of each option. Fifth, this information will be brought back to the trustees and faculty for decisions or additional consideration. This process might iterate for a while before landing on a desirable outcome.

While this hypothetical procedure seems straightforward, it would be unlikely to unfold that way in practice. Exploring mergers, acquisitions, and closures is difficult, even wrenching, and entails debates with many constituencies and many more agendas. Often, these explorations begin in highly confidential settings (e.g., just among the trustees or the executive committee of the board). Once they move beyond these confines, the pace is often rapid, due to the urgency involved. In these circumstances, even the most inclusive intentions often are impinged by necessity. As Professor McCay, of the New Hampshire Institute of Art, whose 121-year-old institute completed its merger with larger New England College in the summer of 2019, said to the *New York Times*, "As in an arranged marriage, there's not much time for the faculty and staff to 'date' . . . It only happens after the appropriate parental authorities have negotiated the legal and financial aspects. And the two individuals then have to hope that their personalities will mesh."[11] That is why the president and board chair have to be equal to the task of leading such a process.

The previous example presupposes a board or faculty even willing to discuss options of such magnitude. The mere mention of the discussion (even if it leads to no action) may set off alarm bells that cannot be "un-rung." One way to avoid this stigma is to make these sorts of discussion routine. This might take the form of a recurring board agenda item, perhaps along with the annual audit. It could even be rolled into the institutional assessment process. Making it routine would accomplish a number of things: it would destigmatize the process and make it more thorough and open; it would give the institution's leadership a mandate to discuss options with the leadership of other institutions; and finally, it would reduce the necessity for confidentiality, which overrides the normal shared governance process. In the same spirit, other strategic analyses could be made more regular, perhaps aligned with strategic planning or reaccreditation cycles. Another benefit of this approach is to blunt the notion that certain options or pathways are not possible or even worthy of exploration. Quite the opposite, an academic community committed to freethinking, thorough analysis, and healthy skepticism ought to able to consider difficult strategic options and choices. The shared governors should take the lead, not throw up bulwarks.

Thankfully, most institutional measures and assessments are not of this magnitude. That does not make them any less important. Presidents and provosts should work to establish a deliberate culture of assessment. Because assessment is the continuous component that runs through every planning effort, it should be established before a college or university develops a strategic plan, responds to an accreditor, or develops a dashboard of metrics for the board of trustees. A culture of assessment leads naturally to a culture of responsibility. It also drives institutional priorities. In 1996, during its reaccreditation, Augustana College was told that its "assessment plan and its implementation [were] not up to the high standards of the rest of the institution."[12] The college spent the next fifteen years working diligently on assessment at every level, but focused particularly on improving student learning outcomes. This work was supported by three grants from the Teagle Foundation. The first, in 2005, addressed student growth in writing, critical thinking, and civic engagement. The second, in 2008, supported the building of a senior capstone experience. The third grant, in 2009, focused on how faculty work can be restructured to allow for more active, experiential learning strategies. This work and its associated assessment were embodied in successive strategic plans, fundamentally changing the direction of the college. In a 2010 convocation speech, Augustana's president, Steven C. Bahls, said, "This is part of a shift in students and their families asking about value and outcome, and that is precisely what we have been working on for the past 10 years at Augustana: shifting to an outcomes-based education, assessing student learning, and providing more internship, research and international experiences—all of which lead to great outcomes . . . we need to develop principles for prioritizing projects on campus with the overriding objective of improving student learning outcomes."[13]

When the National Institute for Learning Outcomes Assessment did a case study of Augustana, they noted four lessons learned. First, build a group of campus assessment experts, including faculty and senior administrators, who are charged with monitoring program reviews. Second, create an atmosphere of transparency around the sharing of assessment information, including the underlying nonconfidential data. Third, focus on smaller, more manageable assessment projects, remembering Voltaire's wisdom that the best is the enemy of the good. These measures may ultimately be combined into a more omnibus assessment system, but that does not have to be the initial goal. Fourth, and finally, programs can learn from one another. The outcome of a program, successful or unsuccessful, often drives future programs and even institution-wide efforts. This is also true of assessment rubrics and protocols. They tend to increase in efficacy and scope as they are refined over multiple projects. The more a college or university focuses on measuring success, the better it will get at assessment.

The same goes for the board of trustees. Their oversight role as fiduciaries is complicated by their seeing only snapshots in time. The annual audit is a good example of this effect. Every fall the auditors meet with the board to discuss the financial health of the institution. The audit may reveal that the institution is in excellent shape or great peril, but it is unlikely to reveal how it got there. Because new trustees often have no historical basis to draw upon, many institutions have adopted the use of a so-called dashboard, with visual and numeric performance indicators of factors ranging from finance and enrollment to student success and athletics. Dawn Terkla, who collected samples from sixty-six public and private institutions,[14] found that the number of indicators varied widely, from as few as three to as many as sixty-eight. Three-quarters had a single dashboard, and the rest had multiple dashboards (e.g., student indicators, financial indicators, academic indicators, athletics indicators). She noted that "the best dashboards were organized by categories or topics, and included useful contextual information like trend data for the institution or average scores for a comparison group. Some included a goal or target, or arrows showing the direction of change and whether that was good, bad, or neutral." The value of a good dashboard is really borne out in time. Trustees can quickly look backward to prior dashboard reports to see overall trends and trajectories. They can also scrutinize the latest report for similar deviations. This provides them with continuity and perspective, without their having to do the exhaustive analysis on their own.

Institutional, strategic, and programmatic assessments are all important, but so are individual performance reviews, at all levels. From a leadership perspective, assessments of the president and the trustees themselves are the most significant. Presidents should be eager to undergo a reasonable annual review, based on the results of clear goals set the previous year, related to strategic, advancement, and continuous improvement. The board of trustees or a subset thereof, such as a compensation committee or an executive committee, is charged with this task. Its members need to take full responsibility for the review and be proactive in their work. It is neither fair nor effective to expect the president to do the bulk of the work, as sometimes occurs. It is also inappropriate to involve other members of the president's senior staff, except in providing data and basic analysis, with the president completely in the communications loop. Trust and mutual respect are as important as candor in this process. The goal is to provide the president with useful feedback, which increases the likelihood of success in the coming year. If performance problems are apparent, then the goal should be to help the president improve. If these problems are beyond repair, then the process of exiting the president should be done with great care, so as not to harm either the reputation of the president or the institution.

The board chair and trustees should be equally diligent about reviewing themselves. Trusteeship is about doing the work of governing well. Trustees who do not attend meetings, who are not well prepared, or who avoid work assignments are not effective trustees. The board should have clearly stated expectations of each trustee and regular reviews conducted by either the full board or a trusteeship or nominations committee. The chair should be an enthusiastic and vocal advocate for this process. Like the presidential review, these assessments should be honest and open, the goal being to improve individual trustees and the overall functioning of the board. If a trustee is found to be particularly problematic, then there should be mechanisms to drive improvement or alternately to exit the trustee. Again, as with the president, this should be done carefully, especially since many trustees are alumni, major donors, or have extensive relationships with the institution's many constituencies. Nevertheless, dysfunction must be addressed and rectified; the board's effectiveness depends upon it.

US Supreme Court Justice Potter Stewart famously wrote of pornography, "I shall not today attempt further to define the kinds of material I understand to be embraced within that shorthand description, and perhaps I could never succeed in intelligibly doing so. But *I know it when I see it*."[15] The same could be said for many people's notion of success and failure. However, it is rare that institutional and individual improvement is black and white. Continuous improvement is driven cyclically and iteratively by a process of measurement and assessment that informs changes and further action. While the precision of the process may vary greatly, it will only be refined through continued diligence and commitment to improvement. The leadership has to truly embody this commitment if it is to flourish throughout the organization. The leadership should also be committed to making decisions, sometimes very difficult ones, to continue to drive improvement forward. The president, provost, and board chair must work together toward these common goals of institutional improvement and strategic success. It is arguably the most important activity that these three leaders do in concert. Being successful and measuring success go hand in hand. College and university leaders who understand this fact will have a competitive advantage in an increasingly difficult market and will serve and advance the mission of the institution with greater breadth and effectiveness.

8

Innovation

When it comes to Americans' understanding of innovation, tech innovators such as Steve Jobs, Elon Musk, and Bill Gates tend to dominate the imagination. These outsized inventors are, in fact, poor examples of innovation. Although the products they have created may shape our popular imagination of innovation, these inventors were seeking breakthroughs, not progressive improvement via management processes. True innovation is the process of creating an improvement that can be inserted into an existing management or operational practice. While breakthroughs are rare, especially on American college campuses, progressive or continuous improvement is a deeply held tradition in the liberal education upon which most of them are founded. In fact, accreditors base much of their review on an institution's willingness and commitment to a process of quality enhancement. As such, a higher education institution should be a vehicle to support a culture of innovation on its campus. For accreditors, innovation is also tied to assessment because assessment determines the success of the practices and processes under which a college or university operates.[1]

Leadership of most colleges approach innovation with a remarkable naiveté, and the concept of innovation can mean something different on almost every campus. Some institutions link innovation to the production of products driven by faculty research and scholarship interests. The use and application of the word *innovation* also results in a complicated array of initiatives across the campus. To support innovation, many campuses now have an administrative position dedicated to executing it.[2] It is difficult to lead on innovation when the definition of innovation is murky, ill defined, or nonexistent. Yet innovation looms large over the future of most colleges and universities. American higher education must adapt continuously for its institutions to become sustainable. Those that fail to innovate may have a different timetable before an existential crisis hits, but their future rests in large part on their ability to innovate their way through the twenty-first century. Innovation is not about how much money you have in the bank, how impressive your research faculty and staff might be, or whether the leadership folds a call for innovation into the college's strategic plan. Happily, most tuition-driven institutions have survived because they innovated their way to change and adapted to the realities of what faced them throughout their history.[3]

In theory, American higher education would seem to be an ideal breeding ground for innovation. Colleges and universities are the repositories of our collective knowledge, cultural traditions, and much of the imaginative and original thinking in society. These institutions are governed by process, particularly in their on-campus interactions. There are a group of internal systems that operate in interrelated harmony, more or less, despite the territorial claims of departmental and office fiefdoms. But if process is king on a college campus, the shared governance that manages it can deleteriously impact the efficiency of management and operations by creating and fostering a pervading sense of cultural inertia.[4] There is a frustrating irony among leaders who work with brilliant people with fresh ideas but are guided and limited on campus by process-driven roadblocks. Cultural inertia can dampen synergy and impede a culture of innovation on a college campus looking to adapt programs and facilities to new social, cultural, and economic realities.

As we noted in chapter 2, on strategic planning, companies like General Electric, Disney, and Hughes represent good illustrations of innovative systems that are seeking continuous improvement. These examples demonstrate that innovation is the process of creating an improvement and inserting it into an existing enterprise. If colleges and universities are working overtime to adapt to a radically shifting environment, they must first agree on what they mean by innovation. This agreement assumes that the institution will remain true to its mission and celebrate its rich history. By looking forward, innovation also makes it possible for higher education institutions to look and behave differently in the future from the way they operate today. Recent books on innovation in higher education have a few critical points in common: they acknowledge the outmoded institutional structure of colleges, which is rooted in a nineteenth-century model, and they advocate for urgent change in the face of rising tuition costs, increasing reliance on contingent faculty, and a dwindling ability to effectively prepare students for the modern economy and global issues. Michael Crow and William Dabars's *Designing the New American University* is one of the best-known treatments of how colleges can address these issues published within the last five years.[5] As the title suggests, the coauthors posit a new model for universities based on the changes Crow implemented as president of Arizona State University. Their proposed new model is more attuned to improvements in undergraduate teaching by employing cost-effective teaching technologies, focusing on research with clear public value, and demonstrating greater responsibility to local communities.

The concept of disruptive innovation developed by Clayton Christensen of the Harvard Business School has generated extraordinary levels of thinking about technology-led innovation in higher education, including Christensen's own *The Innovative University: Changing the DNA of Higher Education.*[6] More recently, Richard DeMillo chronicled how Silicon Valley entrepreneurs radically changed higher education by providing lower-cost teaching technologies, specifically, Massive Open Online Courses (MOOCs). In his *Revolution in Higher Education*, DeMillo argued that this major disruption has already happened, notably in 2012, which DeMillo called "the Magic Year."[7] His "small band" of scholar-entrepreneurs includes Daphne Koller and Andrew Ng, who founded Coursera; Sebastian Thrun, who pioneered Udacity; and Ben Nelson, who created the Minerva Project. Nelson is also the coeditor of *Building the Intentional University*, which focuses on Minerva. On the whole, these techno-centered innovation narratives focus on the imminent, perhaps inevitable, promise that new teaching technologies will deliver the curriculum in cheaper and more widely accessible ways.

As David Staley points out in the introduction to *Alternative Universities*, Teressa Sullivan's resignation from the University of Virginia was forced by a board that perceived her as too slow to respond to the inevitable revolution promised by tech disruptions like MOOCs.[8] Although the success and impact of MOOCs are debatable, Staley notes that they obviously have not made brick and mortar colleges obsolete. Instead, the assumption that technology will disrupt higher education may be waning, and we may be facing an existential crisis based on "a poverty of ideas about what universities can become."[9] To that end, Staley presents ten bold utopian, but feasible opportunities that might shape the future of higher education, ranging from micro-colleges to the "Polymath University," where students major in three different disciplines. He also reminds us that there have been several key moments of innovation in American higher education, including the German research university of the nineteenth century, land-grant universities, the experimental colleges of the early twentieth century, and the development of community colleges in the twentieth century.

Building on the origins and history of American higher education, Cathy Davidson's *The New Education* and Stephen M. Gavazzi and E. Gordon Gee's *Land-Grant Universities for the Future* offer visions for the academy that are less about disruption and focus on playing to established strengths in innovative ways.[10] In *The New Education*, for example, Davidson advocates for rethinking general education that "is expansive, deep, reflective, analytical, critical, creative, technological, sometimes combining a preprofessional application with a liberal arts grounding."[11] Her teaching-focused vision draws on examples from elite research intuitions as well as community colleges, whereas Gavazzi and Gee describe a "land-grant fierce" approach, which advocates for those institutions to return to their original mission of closely serving their local communities and states. Another theme that many of these recent books have in common is the advice to institutions not to engage in "Harvard worship" or attempt to emulate elite institutions. As we have argued throughout this book, leadership must lean into its own unique brand and strengths and support its local communities, regions, and state-specific goals.

If there is a commitment to innovation, continuous improvement can be driven by opportunity and need, or both. Opportunity is an especially attractive driver. The rising angst and growing anger about college indebtedness, now at $1.6 trillion dollars and rising annually, mandates that American higher education find some way to control costs, rebrand its perceived value, and retain its hold in market share, as new mechanisms for delivery emerge, ebb, and flow.[12] The deep recession, changes in modalities precipitated by the COVID-19 pandemic, rising socioeconomic inequality, and racial unrest have only exacerbated and intensified this trend. Collaborations on any level—programs, research, student life, resource-sharing, and other means—provide attractive vehicles to support the kind of innovation that improves management and reinforces systematic, continuous growth and improvement. There is additional value in the need to innovate. Innovation requires careful stewardship of resources, often seen narrowly on most every campus as balancing the operations budget. It can be bottom-up or top-down, but the most effective institutions have processes in place that encourage, capture, and embed good ideas at every level.

While good ideas and innovations may be generated internally, another important driver for innovation can be what's going on with peer and competitor institutions, related industries like medical care and hospitality, or systematic improvements made by business and industry generally.[13] On the business side of college operations, for example, advancement divisions have long looked to other institutions for innovation. While their national professional association is officially known as the Council for the Advancement and Support of Education (CASE), the industry joke has long been that the acronym stands for "Copy and Steal Everything."[14] This is not a negative take; rather, ideas, approaches, and processes that work for one institution are likely to work for another. Beyond the innovation itself, the way that innovation is implemented at another institution may be especially helpful, saving a great deal of time and money and avoiding missteps and aggravation. The danger is, of course, that if adopted universally across higher education, the innovation may not produce the level of continuous improvement that separates institutions from one another.

Who is in charge of innovation? How do you manage innovation? No matter what the scale or complexity of an institution, it is unlikely that the president, board, or faculty chair should lay individual claims to lead innovation across campus. It is equally unlikely that the chief financial officer or one of the staff should bear principal responsibility for it. CFOs ration budgets, but they may be limited in their ability to see how the pieces fit together, especially on the academic side of the house. The same may be said of provosts and chief academic officers. Innovation may take center stage and also function in a back-of-the-house setting. Innovation is not relegated to either/or—academics or administration; rather, it fosters the synergy and creative climate colleges and universities need to become more efficient and creative and to adapt to what they cannot foresee. While there is no single individual or group with the sole responsibility for innovation, the drive to support it must begin at the top. Board chairs must speak clearly and focus the agenda. The agenda must, in turn, reflect where the board wants the institution to be, not where the institution is. To be effective, boards must streamline their operational discussions to focus on how to create a climate for continuous improvement in which creativity and an entrepreneurial spirit will flourish. They must marry innovation to campus culture and challenge the administration and faculty to seek continuous improvement with measurable standards. They must insist that good ideas cannot exist in fiefdoms or in isolation in administrative offices, laboratories, and classrooms across campus.

Boards must use their key oversight responsibilities to insist that a culture of innovation emerge.[15]

Faculty also has a critical role to play. Led by the provost or chief academic officer, the faculty must embrace innovation as opportunity. This will require two important changes on campus. The first is to ensure complete transparency about how colleges innovate so that the campus, especially the faculty, recognize that efforts to create improvements and insert them into management practice are enlightened, not a thinly disguised effort to further ration a tight budget. Faculty must also avoid assuming that new breakthroughs adopted into management practices are the equivalent of an administration picking winners and losers. To do so, a culture of innovation must build upon a basis of transparency. The key stakeholders cannot enforce a culture of innovation without a campus community willing to understand and embrace it. There are examples of innovation emerging from a campus committed to innovation in every type of higher education setting. Historically, many research universities grew from land-grant colleges. Four-year campuses, public and private, seeking to link their liberal arts tradition to workforce preparation, introduce new professional and technical programs typically grounded in a liberal arts tradition. Community colleges are in many respects the most innovative and most responsive to developing new programs suited to emerging needs in American society.

The president has the responsibility to present the case for innovation on campus. Presidents have a number of valuable tools at their disposal. The first is their support from the board. Board chairs and presidents must agree on how an institution will be managed and live its mission. But they must also look ahead and make certain they provide the president with the management tools that will shape and enable the execution of a strategic plan. When these "rules of the house" have been determined, presidents will have the authority within shared governance to create an innovative climate. It may take time, but the rules of the game are in full view. Once established, all stakeholder groups, including the trustees, must follow them. Trustees can also play an important role by providing critical seed funding to promote innovation that links to operations and management practices.[16]

Presidents also have the ability to create a culture of innovation. They can change out their staff, repurpose it, and bring in players better suited to a changing campus climate. In schools governed by cultural inertia and fiercely protected fiefdoms, new presidents need to worry, not only if inherited senior staff can move to an innovation agenda, but also if they are even willing to do so. One special concern is that they will use their friends, especially trustees with whom many have long relationships, to maintain their position, arguing against what they perceive to be radical change.[17] Presidencies are short term and growing more so each decade. Colleges cannot create a culture of innovation simply by mandating it; they must guard against established staff who fear too much change despite the growing need to adapt to shifting circumstances. Presidents must have the players in place who understand innovation and are willing to make it work, and they should not be afraid to replace senior staff who oppose innovation, provided that the board does not interfere in personnel decisions.

As authors of the strategic plan and principal spokespersons for their institution, presidents have a special responsibility to foster and promote innovation. Presidents have numerous opportunities to present their case for a culture of innovation to stakeholders across all campus constituencies. The beauty in this task is that selling innovation carries with it a fresh approach that can create a sense of palpable momentum on campus, which is critical to building support for a strategic agenda to foster a culture of innovation. Stakeholders understand the intersection between fresh ideas, practices and programs, efficient management, and continuous improvement, supporting prudent use of existing resources, and the capacity to incorporate new approaches and ideas. For many of them, selling innovation demonstrates that presidents are also successfully crafting a vision for their institutions.

Presidents can create a culture of innovation by using the financial resources of an institution wisely. The little-known fact beyond the college gates is that so many costs led by labor, financial discounting, debt repayment, capital maintenance, and improvement and depreciation are fixed; there is little discretionary money available to support development of an innovative campus. There is even less to drive these innovations down to colleges, departments, and offices. Working with their senior staffs, especially the CFO, presidents must find a way to create a pool of money to invest in innovation. They cannot create an innovative culture on campus without the resources to reward progressive improvement and the breakthroughs it creates. This can be done by repurposing existing resources and locating new sources of support. Trustees committed to change can play a pivotal role in financing it. Further, these commitments also tie back directly to the type of president—especially a strategist—they appointed to lead the institution.

This is where a close cooperative bond between the president and the chief financial officer shows its worth. Any effort to support a systemic incorporation of innovation on a college campus requires new budgeting approaches, which can themselves ultimately be good examples of innovation. The easiest way is to reserve increasing amounts of discretionary funds each year, until the amount reserved begins to match the public pronouncements made about the continuous improvements on a college campus. A second approach is to create the efficiencies and economies of scale supported by innovative practices, protocols, and programs that effectively self-fund continued innovation. A third approach is to seek new sources of revenue to support innovation as part of the broader strategic plan. Colleges and universities may also be able to find the financial resources to fund innovation by going beyond incremental savings to ask foundational questions about what they should no longer do, thereby freeing up significant savings for more strategic continuous improvements to drive innovation. And finally, colleges can actively seek strategic alliances with other institutions, corporations, and foundations to increase revenue for targeted initiatives.

Any effort to create a culture of innovation must, of course, be enthusiastically supported by the faculty. Many large research universities, for example, MIT and Stanford, have internalized their innovative cultures to reflect the mission articulated when they formed. Others, such as Carnegie Mellon and Arizona State, brand themselves on their basis of their management acumen as centers of innovation. Still others, including Harvard, NYU, the University of Rochester, and Rowan, are in serious internal discussions about how to move more rapidly and fully to an innovative culture. In every case, the role of the faculty in supporting innovation will determine how well institutional leaders reimagine how to adapt management practices with continuous improvement. As the scale and complexity diminishes, small- and mid-sized colleges can take a lead in developing innovation. It is true that the faculty are typically traditionalists. Many contribute on their campuses to the sense of cultural inertia that exists, especially if supported by endowments whose drawdowns mask much deeper problems about long-term adaptability.

In a sense, however, the existential crisis that many of these institutions face is also a blessing disguised by the crisis. Tuition-driven institutions must adapt more quickly because they lack the resources to delay their need to act to remain viable. For these institutions to become sustainable, they must move beyond cuts, delays, or cancellations of promising new initiatives. Their only choice is to act, and the sooner the better. The necessity of the present may lead many of them to innovate their way to a more sustainable future. At many national conferences lately, organizers are developing panels, sessions, and meetings to address how to innovate toward a sustainable future, set against a backdrop of collapsing demographics, changing consumer preferences, and unsustainable college operational models.[18]

Innovation is not the preserve of the rich institution or the research university. In fact, innovation can occur in any setting. One can fill management graveyards with the bad ideas in higher education. Like other industries, higher education has its share of flash-in-the-pan moments. The recent craze over MOOCs provides a good example.[19] Further, some ideas that use to be new have now become part of the fabric of American higher education. To illustrate, high-speed broadband networks were once the province of elite research universities but are now more akin to electricity as a utility on the modern campus. The incorporation of innovative ideas has changed the way colleges and universities operate in countless ways. Enrollment management is a good example. Few institutions administer financial aid without significant predictive analytical models. These models have been around for a generation or more. Many are effective, but there is a sense that some of the financial aid modeling is tired and repetitive, failing to account, for example, for student life interests, which directly affect acceptance, retention, and graduation rates. It may be that financial aid modeling itself will undergo a transformation and include new variables to improve predictability.

Technology has also fundamentally changed the way that faculty convey their wisdom to students, shaping both the communication and process by which students acquire it. College officials communicate via social media and numerous other venues that give them instant platforms.[20] It is unclear what impact technology might have on pedagogy moving forward, especially in the wake of the COVID-19 pandemic, which forced many institutions to offer classes online. The cumulative result of the incorporation of innovative platforms, programs, ideas, and models into efforts to continuously improve a campus has generally made them better and more responsive places.

Risks also accompany innovation. Without setting clear parameters, innovation can be expensive, especially when mistakes are made. There are two obvious dangers. The first is when the principal stakeholders are not fully aligned on how to create a culture of innovation with established parameters. The board, administration, and faculty must agree on why and how to create a culture of innovation, linking it to a campus-wide strategy that creates greater long-term sustainability. Not every good idea supports continuous improvement. Others do, but they may be an unnecessary or impractical fit. The best way to avoid competing claims is to make certain that there is ongoing discussion across the campus on how to lay the groundwork for innovation. Put in other terms, creating a culture of innovation is hard work. The payoff is enormous, of course, because the ability of an institution to survive will depend on how it can link its improvements in a rapidly changing competitive higher education environment.

A number of campuses have established "innovation czars," sometimes presented as all-knowing gurus, based upon the particular level of experience that landed them their job. In other examples, the president serves as the chief exponent of innovation. If innovation is simply a management tool, designed to create efficiencies, CFO's often take the lead. If innovation is synonymous with marketing fresh ideas, provosts step forward to lead the charge. But whatever the internal decision, there is always the need for a traffic cop. Presidents have a wide range of responsibilities that make it almost impossible to keep innovation alive and vibrant among campus constituencies. It always comes back to how innovation is perceived and whether its importance is fully communicated across campus. In an atmosphere of missed enrollment targets and constrained resources, colleges must be willing to tie their futures to innovation or risk losing their relevance in the eyes of stakeholders and the general public. Why must colleges commit to innovation? Because they have no choice.

If innovation makes colleges more dynamic and adaptable, it can also provide the synergy that makes colleges more sustainable going forward. As such, someone needs to be in charge. Presidents are simply too busy and typically have a different set of professional skills. Most are ill-suited to direct the day-to-day interactions, enforce the parameters that govern innovation on campus, and serve as traffic cop for the various proposals on how to innovate on campus, especially since these can come from a large number of internal and external sources. But presidents must also not mistake the administrative and management assistance necessary to establish and support innovation as an opportunity to diminish their attention to it. Each presidential type—presiders, change agents, and strategists—must learn how to govern within the culture of innovation. It's often especially difficult for presiders and change agents to embrace innovation, but the best of them see it as a way to reinforce their own sense of how the campus community should develop.

Depending upon how an institution organizes the flow of innovation, the traffic cop should report either to the provost or the president and work closely with the chief finance officer, if only because innovation can be expensive, even if the end result occasionally may be to drive down costs. The traffic cop, often a vice president for innovation, has one basic responsibility. She or he must make sure that all stakeholders are aligned to support a culture of innovation that points directly to the strategic plan. Strategic plans often include 30,000-foot overviews about change aimed at making the institution a more sustainable place. If the stakeholders fall out of line or the culture that supports innovation does not energize the strategic plan, then the innovation within campus culture becomes irrelevant to the ultimate goal of continuous improvement. The arrangement between the traffic cop and the CFO must work well or efforts to innovate will fail as the turf wars erupt between them or with other offices on campus.

It is important to have a traffic cop and a home for innovation, but to create such a culture, college stakeholders must capture the energy that comes with innovation. To begin, it is necessary that the institution fund the effort. Innovation cannot exist in a vacuum. College stakeholders must take the lead to determine how to create a culture that supports it. If good ideas create significant efficiencies, for example, those who innovated successfully should receive at a minimum a reward for their success. Their reward should not be based upon the good idea but on how that idea fits into a carefully defined, well-articulated program of continuous campus improvement. And since innovation can emerge from any aspect of college operations, programs, and practices, it is especially useful to recognize staff as well as faculty. Campus culture involves every constituency and is not something created in isolation by the faculty. A culture of innovation flows from an inclusive campus community, one that sees itself as part of an evolving institution and understands that the challenges a college faces can only be met by teamwork. A successful culture of innovation links innovation, adaptability, and sustainability to the professional qualities that drive it.

The goal of any emergent institution adjusting to the new realities of higher education must be to create a culture in which innovation is the norm across program, practices, and protocol. Think of it this way: colleges and universities measure their success in creating a culture of innovation when the community fully embraces innovation as a directional guide in their path going forward. The campus community knows and appreciates that innovation is the dynamic that shifts them toward sustainability when innovation is seen by its members as moving from the unique to the ubiquitous. Innovation is no longer exceptional, but expected. The culture must lay the foundation for innovation that has a lasting presence on campus. It must survive changes in leadership at all levels, economic downturns, shifting demographics, shifts in strategy, and pandemics. To ensure that the culture be safeguarded, it must be embedded in all campus operations. There must also be standards by which to measure progress. These standards are the tangible evidence necessary to keep alignments among campus constituencies in place.

The need to foster and sustain a climate of innovation may be promoted by the administration and led by the president, but the ultimate responsibility to keep innovation alive in the long term rests more with the board and the faculty. Presidents come and go. New administrations take office with different priorities and understandings of what innovation means on a campus. They often have a need to create a climate that more closely parallels the experience the new president brings to the job. Boards that work well have a longer perspective, however, and set an innovation agenda that bridges the gap across administrations. The faculty also play a significant role because they are charged with maintaining the traditions that support the continued evolution of their institution. This means that executive search firms must understand fully what kind of culture exists, thereby determining from the outset what administrative leader they will need. That's not to say that a culture of innovation cannot exist using different languages and approaches, but the failure to innovate makes a college or university less adaptable. It subjects the institution to fits and starts if new leadership takes over and fails to build the continuity to support innovation. In this sense, innovation is a cultural commitment set within the broader context of continuous improvement.

That said, innovation is not the preserve of the strategist president alone, although these presidents are perhaps most suited to foster it.

Strategic visionary presidents typically see innovation as a tool that help them encourage the campus to think less about tactics and more about their end game. Yet all can advocate for innovation. Change agents and presidents face similar circumstances. Both types of leader foster innovation because it serves their purposes to institutionalize continuous improvement. The trick for them is not to do damage to a culture already in place in pursuit of a singular vision. It's even more simplistic to imagine that presidents preserve and protect the status quo, which makes them adverse to a culture of innovation. In fact, presider presidents may work diligently and quite successfully to foster the culture that supports slow, methodical improvement. The biggest threat from them is that they may not do enough to support innovation, not fully appreciating that innovation supports the existing campus culture once the campus community fully commits to it.

That's not to say that only a culture of innovation establishes parameters that define acceptable limits to continuous improvement. There are many avenues on a college campus to support orderly institutional growth, much of which brings improvements. Boards can set policies that impact an agenda. Presidents can offer a strategic vision that may be compelling and quite specific, even if looking at the future from 30,000 feet above ground. Faculty can grow the academic program incrementally, and CFO's can fund all these initiatives. Most higher education institutions have long traditions, approach the future incrementally, and live by annual budgets, especially on tuition-driven campuses. Despite the recent rise in mergers, sales, closures, and acquisitions, most colleges and universities will survive, even if survival means kicking the proverbial can down the road. The open question is whether they will remain relevant.

At the same time, faculty, staff, and students can be creative and inventive without being innovative. An enrollment dean can adopt a new financial aid model, for example, without fully using the model to impact admissions and retention, especially retention. Further, there's also the danger that innovation can become a captured term to indicate a way to improve that becomes rigid and fossilized going forward. The campus community may choose to support what it has, even if the culture of innovation no longer relates to the process by which an institution improves and grows. To prevent this possibility, college campuses must continuously find a way to speak as a community to how innovation moves the campus forward, looking for new strategies and tactics to permit the culture of innovation to evolve as a dynamic and living force, driving a campus toward an end articulated by a good strategic plan. The lasting value of an innovative culture is that it internalizes improvement to channel creativity toward a future that best addresses where a campus can reasonably head.

You can sense a culture of innovation when you visit a college campus. It feels fresh, dynamic, and exciting. There is a common commitment on these campuses that goes beyond efforts to fund quality and foster a sense of history and tradition. Innovation brings to a campus a refined sense of itself, in which the discussion focuses as much on the future as the present. These colleges and universities are often demanding places to work because the expectations are high. They are also typically the best places to imagine the future because the climate supports innovation and change. This is something that the board, administrative, and faculty leadership must recognize as a commitment to good governance. It can also be a unifying factor, especially when determining priorities within an operating budget, fundraising campaign, and endowment drawdown. One of the best features of an innovative campus is that it provides a common framework for discussion about what makes a college or university unique.

The current social, cultural, political, fiscal, demographic, and consumer crises necessitate a plan that will shape a more sustainable future. The tuition-driven model that has guided higher education since the end of World War II is no longer sufficient to move the agenda in the twenty-first century. The failure to innovate may mean the failure to survive for some colleges because they simply waited too long to adapt. In the 2018/19 academic year, the average tuition discount rate for first-time full-time freshmen at private, nonprofit four-year institutions reached a record high of 52.2%.[21] For a few of these colleges, there may be enough good will, endowment, and alumni backing to ignore the question. For most, however, it's not about the money and alumni backing. Their stakeholders worry about three interconnected issues: adaptability, sustainability, and relevance. Creating an innovative climate can make colleges and universities better places. If they are better, their strengths may also make them more adaptable, and if they adapt, they will be more sustainable. But ultimately what defines the value of innovation to a college community is relevance. Innovation is a cross-campus cultural commitment to improve and be better at fulfilling the institution's mission. Innovation is also the foundation upon which mission, history, strategy, and direction rest. On the most creative campuses, a culture of innovation institutionalizes improvement to answer the question of why they should keep doing what they do and how they can do it better.

9

Why Leadership Matters

A s institutions, colleges and universities are not dinosaurs, but
they require leadership that is equal to twenty-first-century demands. After World War II, rising enrollments, state and federal support, and the perceived value of a college degree fueled the growth of
higher education. There were remarkable instances of innovation and
creativity, but the cultural environment continued to support incre-
mentalism and even inertia. Strategic plans sat on shelves, accreditors
slowly increased demands for assessment, and colleges shied away
from annual strategic assessment reviews that would examine questions of sustainability over the longer term. They looked instead to
solve short- and mid-term problems. Many of them ran as small "mom
and pop" nonprofits, organized on principles that originated in the
1970s and were seldom revisited. When they needed to run more efficiently as businesses, they often failed to do so.

In 2020, the COVID-19 pandemic laid bare the growing crises that
already afflicted American higher education. Administrators scram-
bled to examine budgets, end-of-year accounting and audits, cuts, and
furloughs before deciding how to proceed.[1] This required enormous

behind-the-scenes scenario planning as the virus changed the rules of engagement in unpredictable ways. A few institutions went beyond interim planning to longer-term strategic assessments, but, strikingly, colleges and universities were obviously grossly unprepared for a global pandemic they had never anticipated. Most institutions lacked the resources and reserves to stave off a multiyear pandemic without reimagining how they operated.[2] The pandemic, however, effectively demonstrated one fundamental truth: leadership matters. Our final chapter is a "call to arms" for activist presidents, provosts, and board chairs with solid extensive experience to lead the institutions that create the country's intellectual capital and to build upon their solid academic and residential foundations. Leadership must immediately become more creative, adaptive, and nimble. This process should also include analyses of how to change strategic planning and assessment and blend innovation with traditional structures and practices. It mandates transparency and collaboration—both within the institution and across institutions generally—restating colleges' purpose as economic engines that use their brainpower to drive their regions.

At times colleges and universities can sometimes seem like machines that run by themselves. Since decisions are consensus driven, process oriented, and often independent of timing constraints, process can sometimes mask leadership. Further, colleges and universities are fundamentally different from other businesses. They are academic centers, more akin to small cities than corporations. This gives them a political dimension in which decisions must be carefully delineated by decision-makers and are typically driven by consensus. These decisions are often only as good as the research and thought put into them. In shared governance, there is an acknowledged group of leaders who run higher education as an efficient and compassionate business. The success of their policies depends on whether the leaders are knowledgeable about their roles, respectful of their limitations, and aware of the duties, responsibilities, and the lines they must not cross to move an agenda forward. In higher education, leadership is a communal exercise. The pendulum constantly swings from one leadership group to another, with policy formulation being more like sausage making than anything else. The outcome is only as good as the collective wisdom and willingness of each leadership group to learn its job.

In a time when institutions must confront pandemics, deep recession, and longstanding social injustices, recasting and redefining relationships within the governance structure, starting with the education of key stakeholders, is critical. Boards of trustees, especially those anticipating an existential crisis at their institution, should begin to assess what they will need by understanding their present circumstances. Boards should ask whether they have the right administrative leadership to weather the growing, pandemic-fueled complexity of this time of crisis. Does their current leadership have the best mix of strategy, operational knowledge, and financial expertise to shepherd the college or university through this crisis? If the answer is no (or their president has recently resigned or retired), they should be taking immediate action to secure the leadership that can save them. While the question of how to exercise leadership extends across governance, it starts with choosing the right administrator and team.

The choice of a president is the most important first step. A typical presidential search is a six- to nine-month process, for example, usually beginning in late spring or early summer. It is a kind of protocol-driven academic ritual. The new president is typically announced early in the following year and assumes office in July, roughly twelve to fifteen months after the search started. In the meantime, the board of trustees usually names an acting or interim president. While he or she has the authority of the presidency, the job basically requires that an interim president safeguard the status quo and fulfill the ceremonial obligations of the office. This process is unlike a chief executive search in any other industry. Higher education's "exceptionalism" assumes that a consultative process that includes trustees, faculty, staff, students, alumni, and the community will take longer. Further, the July 1 start date also begins the new academic year. This schedule made sense when traditions served their institutions better, but today expediency is critical to sustainability and in many cases survival.

Traditions are important, especially in higher education. While this elongated process might be defended in a more normal economic environment, it is reckless and even dangerous during a global pandemic and a rapidly deepening economic depression. In these times of crises, trustees must recognize that their fiduciary responsibilities require them to question and take responsibility for how presidential searches are conducted, and selections must be based on the cold, hard facts. Candidates must also fully appreciate the level of stress that exists on the campus, and demonstrate how to deploy strategy and create a vision to shepherd the campus into a future with enormous uncertainty. Search committees, and the boards who accept their recommendations, must be practical and clearheaded about what kinds of candidate best fit the "new normal."

It's also time to seize the practical by linking technology to a clear sense of the type of leadership required in this crisis, which will persist throughout the next decade. It is possible to organize a broad and consultative process that will be supported on campus in a short time frame. To start, search committees can use virtual conference technologies for first-round interviews. This might enable them to base their decision on merit rather than a single performance during a staged, orchestrated, and often artificial airport interview. Search committees can use the same technique to conduct additional rounds of interviews, delegating the final decision to a smaller group, led by a committee chair. They can still consult with key stakeholders, broadly and transparently, throughout this process. Boards can also meet by conference video to debate and ultimately bless the decision.

In the new reality amplified by the pandemic, the board of trustees must bring the new president onto the campus without delay, independent of the academic calendar and traditions. Every college will be operating at a deficit for years to come. Their boards must educate themselves quickly, lean into the hard decisions ahead, and craft a climate for the success of the new president. It's not just a question of modernizing the presidential selection process. As we noted, who and how they choose may be the most important decisions that boards can make in the near future. Time, tradition, and precedent are no longer on their side. Making critical changes goes beyond a new strategic vision or a series of tactical moves designed to ease the crisis. Leadership begins by recognizing that the way leaders are chosen must also change. Most institutions do not have the luxury of time because their resources are so constrained by the near collapse of the tuition-driven revenue model. Even those with significant resources will ultimately be forced to grapple with persistent and difficult issues. The longer they delay, the more resources they will expend to catch up, leaving them with fewer resources when facing the challenges ahead.[3]

The same urgency must also be applied to the other decision-makers. While board chairs are usually chosen for their track record of leadership on key committees—nominations, finance, academic affairs, development—boards of trustees continue to be haphazard in their preparation of new leaders to assume the role of board chair. Sometimes it's simply that money talks, with significant donors taking board leadership positions. For a few of them, a prestigious appointment as board chair is a transactional expectation. For most, more happily, it's a sense of care and duty that fuels their willingness to lead. Whatever the approach, board chairs lead with the wisdom and limitations of their professional backgrounds, but they are seldom trained in the business of higher education. They often fail to grasp that higher education is a unique industry, in which one must first learn the job in order to do it well. As we have noted before, boards are the weakest link in shared governance. While groups like the Association of Governing Boards provide training, the quagmire facing higher education will not allow board chairs to lead successfully if they effectively run in place.[4] There must be a comprehensive and updated process, after which the board chair can lead in an era when the unexpected can produce existential threats to the policies set by the board. For most board chairs, this process begins by figuring out what they do not know.

We believe that American higher education will be buffeted throughout the coming decade by a remake of its function and purpose within a global economy. Boards, and the chairs who lead them, are uniquely positioned to contribute their wealth, wisdom, and insight to the repositioning of America's colleges and universities. For those institutions that succeed beyond the pandemic, how boards choose their leaders and prepare them for their jobs will make a crucial difference, one that cannot be overestimated. As noted earlier, boards have three functions: they appoint, retain, and replace the president; they approve the budget, manage the endowment, and handle the audit; and they set general policy direction. The worst mistake that a board chair, or boards generally, can make is to confuse studious oversight and micromanagement. The COVID-19 pandemic reset the rules of engagement for boards within shared governance, determining what will consume most of their time through much of the next decade. An effective board chair must separate the mundane from the more important work of the board. The administrators manage the daily operations, offer the insight, develop the tactics, and provide the vision for the board to consider. Boards must be far better prepared to do strategic assessments annually, to move beyond daily operations to questions of long-term sustainability.

The board chair must be a seasoned veteran, who appreciates that the role of board chair requires a teacher who can convey to trustees and other stakeholders what matters most to an institution operating in a confusing global environment. There will always be time for history and tradition, but time has run out for inexperienced boards of trustees, led by uninformed board chairs, if the goal is to seek a sustainable college over the next decade. Board chairs cannot simply serve, they must lead in creative and innovative ways. Board chairs must also live the job in a way that demonstrates why leadership matters. The COVID-19 pandemic has forced boards to modernize their operations or face a disruptive institutional decline. It has provided them with an unprecedented opportunity to lead, serving as the bridge between tradition, policy, and sustainability. But boards must also be ever aware of the costs of their actions. Higher education is an extraordinarily competitive environment and is becoming even more so. Boards must protect the dual functions of any higher education institution: academic learning center and economic engine.

The third leg of the three-legged stool of shared governance is the faculty. Colleges will rise and fall depending on how well educated, creative, and goal-oriented their faculty becomes—with an imminent demographic collapse further complicating this course. The provost has the triple responsibility of serving as senior administrator, acting as a liaison between the administration and other key stakeholders, and working as a faculty advocate. The importance of the role the provost plays must not be underestimated. For colleges and universities to become more adaptable, the provost must transparently lead the faculty by acclimating them to the real choices ahead. It's no longer a situation in which the faculty mount a defensive effort to protect their share of a rationed financial pie. Instead, they must be willing participants and collaborators in shaping a program that responds to pressing modern concerns—from pandemics to the failure of the tuition-driven revenue model.

These pandemic-induced changes speak to a massive retooling in the education of key faculty members on broader issues of national education policy. We have argued throughout this book that volunteer trustees are the weakest link in shared governance, generally lacking a deep understanding of how higher education works. They are burdened with an archaic, unwieldy, and process-driven management and organization structure, which often results in ineffective and inefficient decision-making. While different in design, many college and university faculties suffer from some of these same structural weaknesses. Faculty leaders are often brilliant, as you might expect, and can be the driving forces behind innovation and creativity on a campus. But on many campuses, how faculty leadership is chosen is confusing, especially if the leadership is drawn from a weak department administrative structure or is kept weak because administrators fear heightened levels of faculty involvement. On some campuses, there is often little preparation and almost no recognition that comes with faculty leadership. Further, it presupposes that faculty leaders work effectively with provosts, presidents, CFO's, and senior staff, despite the healthy tension that may exist as they manage their turfs.

If faculty leaders are to be as valuable in the future as they need to be, they must be as educated and fully informed as trustees and administrators on the issues likely to affect them. This takes time. It presumes that there is agreement on what these issues are going into the future. Faculty leaders are teachers and researchers—or both, depending upon the institution—but they must also assume new roles that align their knowledge base better with that of trustees and administrators. They must accept that their leadership role goes beyond advocacy on faculty issues to include institution-wide policy set within a hypercompetitive external educational environment. While they must be true to the mission and history of their institution, they cannot see their role as distinct from efforts to promote creativity in a changing and constantly reimagined environment. Without faculty support, colleges and universities cannot hope to remain relevant and sustainable.

Collectively, this stakeholder group of leaders has two important directions to consider going forward. The first is how to foster innovation and creativity and protect the intellectual capital produced on a college campus. There is real complementarity between how to innovate while simultaneously creating efficiencies and economies of scale. One often supports the other. The second area is how to create basic, lasting efficiencies that go beyond furloughs and capping contributions to retirement funds as a way to decrease deficits. This second effort requires a thoughtful reexamination of what an institution can afford and how it should operate in a post-pandemic environment. Stanford's decision in July 2020 to eliminate eleven of its sports after one year to help close a $70 million deficit is a good example.[5] Even at the most highly endowed and financially sound institutions, there must be a reckoning based on common sense. The pandemic can be the catalyst to make changes that would not be tolerated in the incrementalism of their past rules of engagement.

As we noted, stakeholders extend beyond the college gates. Colleges and universities are economic engines that power regional, state, and national economies. Collectively, higher education represents one of the largest and most dynamic American industries, reshaping the economies of large sections of the United States.[6] They provide jobs, economic spin-offs, and add considerably to the tax base, among many other benefits beyond serving the public good. Typically, they are often the largest employers in their region.[7] This has a significant impact on how leadership is exercised and, as we noted, forces decisions among top leadership on how much time should be devoted to outside interests. In the coming decade, leadership will need to work assiduously to build new strategic partnerships with employers, political leaders, and other nonprofits. It is likely that tuition-paying American consumers will demand better employment options for their graduates. It is equally certain that a post-depression workforce will identify key metrics demanded of an educated workforce. Higher education must be prepared to lead in developing these metrics, including promoting the skills made possible only by a good liberal arts education. The leadership must also remember that one of the best ways to protect the core mission of an institution is to emphasize its role as a regional economic engine, which supports the workforce.

American higher education will play a significant role in rebuilding the economy. How leadership handles the role of their institutions as economic engines will determine the level of their support from state and federal politicians, the continued willingness of consumers to see the value in a college degree, and the speed with which their regions recover from the pandemic. It will mean an adjustment in thinking about their future direction, with strategic plans "writ large" to include how colleges and universities relate to where they are located. It also underscores the need to look at these efforts comprehensively when creating strategic partnerships. Higher education cannot thrive without rebuilding economies to create a better social and cultural environment. They must align what their mission statements declare with what America will become. Crises like the COVID-19 pandemic provide opportunities for higher education leaders to guide rebuilding and support social and cultural advances.

This raises the interesting question of how leadership relates to an institution's sustainability. Is the long-term goal simply to preserve the academic integrity of a college that has enough financial stability to survive? Indeed, institutional sustainability must be a given for a college to make lasting inroads and remain relevant. However, in an information-driven global economy, is there an opportunity to emerge from the pandemic and deep recession with a redefinition of what higher education means in the United States? US colleges and universities have always fed off the internal dynamics that match the creation of knowledge with economic development. The academy has had an outsized effect owing to its dual role in the creation and transfer of knowledge in a global economy. Higher education must shape the intellectual, moral, and ethical framework upon which post-pandemic America rebuilds both its economy and its social and cultural parameters. Collectively, US colleges and universities must see past the narrower struggles to ensure their own future, if only because the broader environment will be dynamic and will heavily influence their success.

At this level, higher education must also become more relevant. At present, the economic return on investment is what seems to be the determining factor among consumers, fueled partly by the press. Political polarization restated as a culture war has pulled higher education off what was left of its perch.[8] Leading up to the 2020 presidential election, the United States saw widespread social unrest, demonstrating that the country is an evolving, living experiment full of imperfections and moments of genuine progress. Pivotal moments like this require intellectual, moral, social, and cultural leadership, which has historically been provided by higher education. The solution is not high-minded soapbox speeches about what could or might happen. Instead, what is called for is a serious open dialogue on race and equality. The best assets of a college or university rest with its intellectual capital. This is where college leadership can both think and do, as America reconciles its past with what's ahead.[9]

As we noted in chapter 6, the repositioning of higher education will have a direct bearing on how colleges relate to their regulators. In the absence of increasing state and federal support, it is likely that regional and professional accreditors and state and local governments will move increasingly to regulation as a way to shape higher education's role in American society. The Commonwealth of Massachusetts, for example, has already moved to determine their level of financial sustainability following Mount Ida College's precipitous closing in 2019.[10] Regional accreditors are shifting beyond questions of accountability through their insistence on structured assessment to broader discussions with colleges and universities about institutional effectiveness. The bedrock is eroding under higher education institutions as they respond to new regulator demands. Situations like the pandemic and deep recession will profoundly influence the direction that regulators take, and higher education leadership must have a say in any new directions charted by regulators, no matter how well intentioned.[11] It will undoubtedly mean that these leaders, especially presidents, will need to take a more active role in these discussions. It also suggests a broader definition of advocacy than the earlier focus on tax exemption, regulation, and student aid argued by most higher education trade associations in Washington and state capitals across the country.

The emergence of the higher education community through this third inflection point will also produce other kinds of response. Because the ability of tuition-driven revenue to generate enough support for higher education in the future is uncertain, college and university leaders must also wrestle with the role of collegiate athletics.[12] Historically, athletics have helped build enrollments, alumni support, and donor interest. In larger programs, it has also been an effective branding opportunity. But, as noted in chapter 6, only a handful of Division I programs even break even.[13] As the debate over whether these expenses justify the sticker price charged to students and their families intensifies, leaders will need to account for and occasionally combat those who resist changes in athletic programming. As discussed, there are already fissures between various NCAA divisions driven by the purpose of sports on campus, the regulatory environment, and money. Furthermore, the justification that athletics contributes to provide alternative programming on a well-balanced campus is challenged by new recruiting methods. These new methods link club sports, academic clubs, Greek life, and alternative housing and programming methods into a more robust student life program tied directly to enrollment. Many campus leaders now argue that such programs are instrumental in recruitment and retention, with far lower costs to implement. For some college leaders, participation in an athletic conference may not be the best use of time or resources in the new enrollment environment, which blends technology, online programming, and alternative forms of residential social options.

Planning and execution are the cornerstones of successful higher education leadership. They create a whole that is greater than the two parts. Yet knowing that an institution needs to plan does not make the planning process any easier. In fact, there may not be a process in the academy more fraught with pitfalls for higher education leaders than strategic planning. Successful strategic planning anticipates this friction and structures a process that simultaneously addresses and mitigates it. Shifting from the tactical to the strategic in their operations and ambitions may be the biggest change in how higher education operates. As the oft-cited quote by legendary hockey player Wayne Gretzky, goes, "I skate to where the puck is going to be, not to where it has been." Higher education cannot rest on how it created a sense of its institutional presence in the world. The current, ongoing global crisis has been uniquely disruptive for higher education institutions that rely on international students, a personalized, intimate education, and population-dense environments.[14] Colleges and universities vary, of course, by the scale, purpose, and management of their institutions, but rapidly changing crises, such as a pandemic, are further exacerbated by local, state, and federal political and administrative decisions. The tactical side of their strategic plan must be nimble enough to link the unanticipated to the strategic sense of where they wish to be. It requires an ability to take many small nontrivial actions and tie them into a shared sense of their future—a vision that cannot be lost if the institution is to survive in a post-pandemic world.

American higher education must always be able to move past momentary crises to develop a lasting vision that speaks individually and collectively to the role their institutions play in society. At all costs, they must argue forcefully for the importance of liberal arts traditions, which are the historic bedrock upon which America's support for higher education—indeed, lifelong education—rests. Institutions must also recognize the pivotal role they play in providing a creative economy, with an educated workforce whose skills match society's need. Given the polarization of today's political culture and the impact that new media have had on it, higher education must produce educated citizens who can appreciate the experiment that made the United States republic possible. To accomplish this, higher education leaders must reassert their role as influencers in American society. This begins by realigning and adapting colleges and universities to be centers of innovation, demonstrating progressive improvement in their management process, beginning with how they shape their curriculum. Leadership must also regain some of the credibility it lost and gave away. This will require restatement of why their leadership matters.

Any of the three types of president we have defined can successfully move an institution forward. But our guidance leans strongly toward the strategist over the presider and the change agent. In a world in which the tuition-driven pricing model no longer works, and the pandemic has effectively ended the older ways of doing business, the battle today is a pragmatic one. It's a battle for survival. Those institutions that are most adaptable will likely also be the most sustainable. Others will soldier on, of course, but as much weaker institutions, and sadly, as far less relevant ones.

How college and university leaders reclaim their role in society will be a test of how dominant a cultural and social force higher education will continue to be in America. It begins by choosing where to spend higher education's intellectual and moral capital in the broader society that it serves. In recent years, for example, a few presidents and faculty publicly supported policies, taken principled position on an issue like climate change, or worked on position papers with local, state, and federal political candidates. Some have gone on to public service. But this approach is hardly sufficient today. If higher education leadership matters, then its spokespersons must weigh in with the authority conferred by their office, across multiple venues, on the crises that threaten the continued vitality of democracy. The issues are obvious, including socioeconomic inequality, systemic racism, climate change, and the rise in authoritarianism, among others. Despite the stock market's roller-coaster ride, Main Street and Wall Street have moved in different directions, obscuring and exacerbating the deep, growing economic chasm in which we live. The end of the pandemic will only further expose the rawness of a society still needing to argue that "Black Lives Matter." The political experiment will fail if Americans turn a tin ear to the self-inflicted wounds still untended.

In the mid-twentieth century, higher education leaders Clark Kerr, Theodore Hesburgh, Derek Bok, and others who spoke on matters of national concern, made an impact on how American society evolved. They weighed in judiciously on race, gender bias, the need for public service, economic disparity, and related issues. Americans listened to them. While we can certainly criticize how often, how strong, and how well they served as national arbiters, these leaders made a difference. Throughout this book, we have argued that the best leaders in higher education understand their role on campus and in the larger world. It is critical for the next generation of leaders to recast how they lead more broadly. They must choose how to make their voices heard, carefully of course, whether individually or collectively. Beginning with trustees, the higher education community must understand that cultural commentary free from partisan politics is part of the job of good governance in higher education. When leadership speaks out in an informed and thoughtful way, the higher education community must also applaud their voices, even if they disagree with their arguments. It will take individual courage and some time to effectively groom the next generation of higher education leaders as the rules of engagement inevitably change.

For America's colleges and universities, the stakes are high. Most of its institutions are adaptable and sustainable, but they, too, must also be more relevant to the society they help shape. The balancing act will be how their leadership remains true to its purpose and mission but also accommodates the demands of a twenty-first century workforce. It's not just about adapting new programs and differentiating their curricula from that of their competitors. It's about laying out the case for progressive change where the demands on leadership meet the challenges ahead. If American higher education merely survives, its leaders will have missed the opportunity during this third inflection point to restate the case for why they are essential to the evolution of the American republic. We need a skilled workforce, buttressed by tradition and infused with technology. But what we require most is for the leadership to "get" the obvious. The pandemic demands that higher education evolve and grow in a crisis that so clearly amplifies the need for good leaders. That is why leadership matters in higher education—now more than ever.

Preface

1. The Morrill Act, signed into law by President Abraham Lincoln in 1862, provided each state with thirty thousand acres of federal land for each member of its congressional delegation. Each state sold the land to raise proceeds to fund public colleges. Sixty-nine colleges were funded by these land grants, including Cornell University, the Massachusetts Institute of Technology, and the University of Wisconsin at Madison. Act is number 7 U.S.C. 321 et seq., https://www.law.cornell.edu /uscode/text/7/304; Guy Gugliotta, "New Estimate Raises Civil War Death Toll, *New York Times*, Apr. 3, 2012, https://www.nytimes.com/2012/04/03/science/civil-war-toll -up-by-20-percent-in-new-estimate.html.

2. Christopher P. Loss, "Why the Morrill Land-Grant Colleges Act Still Matters," *Chronicle of Higher Education*, July 16, 2012, https://www-chronicle-com.ez proxy.library.wisc.edu/article/Why-the-Morrill-Act-Still/132877.

3. Johns Hopkins, for example, was founded in 1876 and modeled after the German research university. For more on early American land-grant universities, see Nathan M. Sorber, *Land-Grant Colleges and Popular Revolt: The Origins of the Morrill Act and the Reform of Higher Education* (Ithaca, NY: Cornell University Press, 2018).

4. Brian C. Mitchell and W. Joseph. King, *How to Run a College: A Practical Guide for Trustees, Faculty, Administrators, and Policymakers* (Baltimore: Johns Hopkins University Press, 2018).

5. Emma Whitford, "Pandemic Worsened Public Higher Ed's Biggest Challenges," *Inside Higher Ed*, June 24, 2020, https://www.insidehighered.com/news /2020/06/24/coronavirus-pandemic-worsened-higher-eds-biggest-challenges-new -survey-shows.

6. Jason E. Lane and D. Bruce Johnstone, eds., *Universities and Colleges as Economic Drivers: Measuring Higher Education's Role in Economic Development* (Albany: State University of New York Press, 2012); Scott Andes, "Five Reasons Why 'Downtown Universities' Matter for Economic Growth," Brookings Institution, Oct. 11, 2017, https://www.brookings.edu/blog/metropolitan-revolution/2017/10/11/five -reasons-why-downtown-universities-matter-for-economic-growth/.

7. It became clear in the spring of 2020 that the available predictive-enrollment models used to plan were no longer useful (Hayoung Kim, Charag Krishnan, Jonathan Law, and Ted Rounsaville, "COVID-19 and US Higher Education Enrollment: Preparing Leaders for Fall," McKinsey & Co., May 21, 2020, https://www.mckinsey

.com/industries/social-sector/our-insights/covid-19-and-us-higher-education -enrollment-preparing-leaders-for-fall; spring 2020 surveys of college-bound and enrolled college students indicated that institutions could see a 20% decline in enrollment for fall 2020 (Scott Jaschik, "Colleges Could Lose 20% of Students," *Inside Higher Ed*, Apr. 29, 2020, https://www.insidehighered.com/admissions /article/2020/04/29/colleges-could-lose-20-percent-students-analysis-says).

8. Congress allocated this money to colleges in March 2020 as part of the Coronavirus Rescue Package, also known as the CARES Act.

9. The American Council on Education and other representative from higher education requested $50 billion in relief from Congress in early March 2020 (Nick Anderson and Danielle Douglas-Gabriel, "Colleges Face a Grim Financial Future," *Washington Post*, Mar. 26, 2020, https://www.washingtonpost.com/education/2020 /03/19/coronavirus-crisis-rocks-colleges-higher-education-groups-push-congress -more-than-50-billion-relief/).

10. Nearly half of the respondents to *Inside Higher Ed*'s 2020 survey of chief financial officers said that their institution "should use this period to make difficult but transformative changes in its core structure and operations in the interest of long-term sustainability" (Doug Lederman, "COVID-19's Forceful Financial Hit: A Survey of Business Officers," *Inside Higher Ed*, July 10, 2020, https://www.inside highered.com/news/survey/covid-19s-forceful-impact-shakes-college-business -officers-confidence?utm_source=Inside+Higher+Ed&utm_campaign=380762fd5d -DNU_2020_COPY_02&utm_medium=email&utm_term=0_1fcbc04421-380762fd5d -236215901&mc_cid=380762fd5d&mc_eid=2088872e50.

Introduction

1. Brooks Blevins, *Lyon College, 1872–2002: The Perseverance and Promise of an Arkansas College* (Fayetteville: University of Arkansas Press, 2003), 18.

2. Nelson D. Schwartz, "The Recovery Threw the Middle-Class Dream under a Benz," *New York Times*, Sept. 12, 2018, https://www.nytimes.com/2018/09/12 /business/middle-class-financial-crisis.html.

3. US Census Bureau, "Real Median Household Income in the United States [MEHOINUSA672N]," June 17, 2019, retrieved from FRED, Federal Reserve Bank of St. Louis. https://fred.stlouisfed.org/series/MEHOINUSA672N; Drew DeSilver, "For Most U.S. Workers, Real Wages Have Barely Budged in Decades," *Factank: News in the Numbers*, Aug. 7, 2018, https://www.pewresearch.org/facttank/2018/08 /07/for-most-us-workers-real-wages-have-barely-budged-for-decades/.

4. Schwartz, "The Recovery Threw the Middle-Class Dream under a Benz."

5. Sara Goldrick-Rab, *Paying the Price: College Costs, Financial Aid, and the Betrayal of the American Dream* (Chicago: University of Chicago Press, 2016); National Center for Higher Education Management Systems (NCHEMS), "Percentage of Percent of Family Income Needed to Pay for College," http://www.higheredinfo .org/dbrowser/index.php?measure=44.

6. Harvard University, Financial Report, Fiscal Year 2017, https://finance .harvard.edu/files/fad/files/final_harvard_university_financial_report_2017 .pdf.

7. Anthony DeBarros and Janet Adamy, "U.S. Births Fall to Lowest Level since 1980s; Number of Babies Born has Declined in 10 of the Last 11 Years as Fertility Rate Slumps, *Wall Street* Journal, May 15, 2019, https://www.wsj.com/articles/u-s -births-fall-to-lowest-rates-since-1980s-11557892860; Brady E. Hamilton, Joyce A. Martin, Michelle J. K. Osterman, and Lauren M. Rossen, "Births: Provisional Data for 2018," *Vital Statistics Rapid Release*, May 2019, https://www.cdc.gov/nchs/data /vsrr/vsrr-007-508.pdf.

8. Nathan D. Grawe, *Demographics and the Demand for Higher Education* (Baltimore: Johns Hopkins University Press, 2018).

9. Preston Cooper, "College Enrollment Surges among Low-Income Students," *Forbes*, Feb. 26, 2018, https://www.forbes.com/sites/prestoncooper2/2018/02/26 /college-enrollment-surges-among-low-income-students/#9402e8b293b9. See also Ashley A. Smith, "Study Finds More Low-Income Students Attending College," *Inside HigherEd*, May 23, 2019, https://www.insidehighered.com/news/2019/05/23 /pew-study-finds-more-poor-students-attending-college; Richard Fry and Anthony Cilluffo, "A Rising Share of Undergraduates Are from Poor Families, Especially at Less Selective Colleges," Pew Research Center, May 22, 2019, https://www.pew socialtrends.org/2019/05/22/a-rising-share-of-undergraduates-are-from-poor -families-especially-at-less-selective-colleges.

10. Scott Jaschik, "The 2018 Surveys of Admissions Leaders: The Pressure Grows," *Inside Higher Ed*, Sept. 24, 2018, https://www.insidehighered.com/news /survey/2018-surveys-admissions-leaders-pressure-grows.

11. Aaron D. Purcell, *Arthur Morgan: A Progressive Vision for American Reform* (Knoxville: University of Tennessee Press, 2014), 103.

12. Robert E. Barde, "Arthur E. Morgan, First Chairman of TVA," *Tennessee Historical Quarterly*, 30 (3): 303.

13. Purcell, *Arthur Morgan: A Progressive Vision for American Reform*, 104–5.

14. Ibid., 105–6.

15. Ibid., 111.

16. Barde, "Arthur E. Morgan, First Chairman of TVA," 304.

17. Purcell, *Arthur Morgan: A Progressive Vision for American Reform*, 112.

18. Ibid., 112.

19. Farnsworth Fowle, "Arthur Morgan of Antioch, First T.V.A. Head, Dies," *New York Times*, Nov. 17, 1975, https://www.nytimes.com/1975/11/17/archives/arthur -morgan-of-antioch-first-tva-head-dies-a-college-innovator.html.

20. Thomas M. Hatfield, *Rudder: From Leader to Legend* (College Station: Texas A&M University Press, 2014), 306.

21. Harvard University, *Financial Report, Fiscal Year 2017*, https://finance.harvard .edu/files/fad/files/final_harvard_university_financial_report_2017.pdf.

Chapter 1. Presidents, Provosts, and Board Chairs

1. William G. Bowen and Eugene M. Tobin, *Locus of Authority: the Evolution of Faculty Roles in the Governance of Higher Education* (Princeton, NJ: Princeton University Press, 2015); Robert Scott, *How University Boards Work: A Guide for Trustees, Officers, and Leaders in Higher Education* (Baltimore: Johns Hopkins University Press, 2018), 27–32; Derek Bok, "The Trouble with Shared Governance," *Trusteeship*, Sept.–Oct. 2013, https://agb.org/trusteeship-article/the-trouble-with-shared-governance; John Lachs, "Shared Governance Is a Myth," *Chronicle of Higher Education*, Feb. 6, 2011, https://www.chronicle.com/article/Shared-Governance-Is-a-Myth/126245; Courtney Leatherman, "'Shared Governance' under Siege: Is It Time to Revive It or Get Rid of It?," *Chronicle of Higher Education*, Jan. 30, 1998, https://www.chronicle.com/article/Shared-Governance-Under/99443.

2. On the concept and tradition of academic freedom and the historical development of shared governance, see Neil W. Hamilton, "The American Academic Profession: The Tradition of Academic Freedom and Shared Governance," in Hamilton, *Academic Ethics: Problems and Materials on Professional Conduct and Shared Governance* (Westport, CT: Praeger, 2002), 17–85; "Board of Director's Statement on Shared Governance," Association of Governing Boards of Universities and Colleges, https://agb.org/reports-and-statements/agb-board-of-directors-statement-on-shared-governance; "Shared Governance: Changing with the Times," Association of Governing Boards of Universities and Colleges, accessed May 12, 2019, https://agb.org/reports-and-statements/shared-governance-changing-with-the-times; Susan Pierce, "Shared Governance: Its History and Its Challenges," in Pierce, *Governance Reconsidered: How Boards, Presidents, Administrators, and Faculty Can Help Their Colleges Thrive* (San Francisco: Jossey-Bass, 2014), 1–24.

3. Examples include Colleen Flaherty, "A Violation of Shared Governance," *Inside Higher Ed*, May 8, 2019, https://www.insidehighered.com/news/2019/05/08/aaup-investigation-finds-vermont-law-school-violated-shared-governance-when-it; Sarah Brown and Eric Kelderman, "Margaret Spellings Is Stepping Down at UNC. Will Anyone Want to Replace Her?," *Chronicle of Higher Education*, Oct. 27, 2018, https://www.chronicle.com/article/Margaret-Spellings-Is-Stepping/244946; Jack Stripling, "U. of Virginia's Board Lacked Common Sense, AAUP Says in Scathing Report," *Chronicle of Higher Education*, Mar. 14, 2013, https://www.chronicle.com/article/Virginias-Board-Lacked-Common/137897; Jack Stripling, "Help Wanted: Leader to Restore Students, Finances, and Trust," *Chronicle of Higher Education*, Feb. 13, 2011, https://www.chronicle.com/article/Help-Wanted-Leader-to-Restore/126337. Susan R. Pierce also provides numerous examples, or "cautionary tales," of how the actions of presidents, faculty, and boards can lead to governance failures, in *Governance Reconsidered: How Boards, Presidents, Administrators, and Faculty Can Help Their Colleges Thrive* (San Francisco: Jossey-Bass, 2014), 89–183.

4. Colleen Flaherty, "Faculty Vote of No Confidence at Westfield State," *Inside Higher Ed*, Mar. 15, 2019, https://www.insidehighered.com/quicktakes/2019/03/15

/faculty-vote-no-confidence-westfield-state; Adam Harris, "Who Wants to Be a College President? Probably Not Many Qualified Candidates," *The Atlantic*, Jan. 24, 2019, https://www.theatlantic.com/education/archive/2019/01/how-politics-are -reshaping-college-presidency/581077; Douglas Belkin, "No Confidence: College Faculties Rebel with More Votes against Leadership," *Wall Street Journal*, May 19, 2018, https://www.wsj.com/articles/no-confidence-college-faculties-rebel-with -more-votes-against-leadership-1526727601; Kate Sinclair, "Student Demands: Who's Resigned, What's Renamed," *New York Times*, Feb 3. 2016, https://www .nytimes.com/2016/02/07/education/edlife/student-demands-an-update.html; Alan Greenblatt, "Why Being a University President Isn't a Stable Job Anymore," *Governing*, Dec. 2016, https://www.governing.com/topics/education/gov-university -presidents-resign.html; Susan Svrluga, "Ithaca College President Resigns after Protests over Race Issues," *Washington Post*, Jan. 14, 2016, https://www.washington post.com/news/grade-point/wp/2016/01/14/ithaca-college-president-resigns-after -protests-over-race-issues/?utm_term=.6a2d6fc97e67.

5. Brian C. Mitchell and W. Joseph King, *How to Run a College: A Practical Guide for Trustees, Faculty, Administrators, and Policymakers* (Baltimore: Johns Hopkins University Press, 2018), 3–9.

6. Brian C. Mitchell, "In Face of Failing Financial Model, What's a College to Do?," *Academeblog*, Jan. 19, 2017, https://academeblog.org/2017/01/19/in-face-of -failing-financial-model-whats-a-college-to-do; Brian C. Mitchell, "The Crisis in How We Fund Higher Education," *Huffington Post*, Apr. 5, 2014, https://www .huffpost.com/entry/the-crisis-in-how-we-fund_b_4716259.

7. Although the policies and guidelines of accrediting bodies do not always include explicit language regarding shared governance, they all have expectations related to the governance process, including transparency and the roles of key constituents. The Higher Learning Commission's policy, for example, requires that an institution's "governance and administrative structures promote effective leadership and support collaborative processes that enable the institution to fulfill its mission" and that the "institution has and employs policies and procedures to engage its internal constituencies—including its governing board, administration, faculty, staff, and students—in the institution's governance" (Higher Learning Commission, *Criteria for Accreditation*, https://www.hlcommission.org/Policies /criteria-and-core-components.html). There have been cases of institutions getting warnings from accrediting agencies for failure to comply with shared governance. In 2012, for example, the Southern Association of Colleges and Schools Commission on Colleges issued a formal warning to the University of Virginia for failing to demonstrate compliance with policies regarding governing boards and the faculty's role in governance after the board had tried to force then president Teresa Sullivan to resign.

8. Examples of these conversations include the 2019 CIC President Institute, where the authors, along with Barbara A. Farley, led the session "How to Adapt a College to New Conditions," and the 2019 National Association of College and

University Business Officers conference, which held sessions titled "Planning to Respond: Physical and Virtual Security" and "What Keeps You Up at Night: A Survey of Chief Business Officers."

9. There are a number of published guidelines for new presidents, including Deborah E. Rupp, Cassie Batz, Melissa Keith, Vincent Ng, Rachel Saef, and Alex Howland, "Competencies for State College and University Presidents," American Association of State Colleges and Universities, 2016, https://www.aascu.org/publi cations/CompetenciesforSCUPresidents.pdf; K. Johnson Bowles, "The President's Many Roles," *Inside Higher Ed*, July 1, 2013, https://www.insidehighered.com/advice /2013/07/01/many-roles-and-expectations-college-presidents-essay; W. Kent Barnds, "Leaders for Small Colleges" *Inside Higher Ed*, Feb. 27, 2013, https://www.inside highered.com/advice/2013/02/27/essay-qualities-needed-leaders-small-colleges; Levon T. Esters, Amanda Washington, Marybeth Gasman, et al., "Effective Leadership: A Toolkit for the 21st-Century Historically Black College and University President," https://cmsi.gse.upenn.edu/sites/default/files/MSI_LdrshpRprt_R3.pdf.

10. In 2017, the average tenure of a college president was seven years (American Council on Education, *The American College President, 2017* (Washington, DC: American Council on Education, 2017).

11. Candidates should carefully determine if the presidential profile aligns with what they observe on campus. If the profile does not accurately reflect campus climate, this is a warning sign.

12. The last decade has seen a shift away from open searches for college presidents (see John Thelin, "Games Colleges Play in Presidential Searches," *Inside Higher Ed*, Aug. 22, 2019, https://www.insidehighered.com/views/2019/08/22/should -presidential-searches-be-open-or-closed-opinion; Monica Kast, "Searching in Secret: Hiring Administrators Is Becoming Less Open and Harder to Cover," Student Press Law Center, Aug. 2, 2018, https://splc.org/2018/08/secret-admin-searches; Celeste Watkins-Hayes "The Pick and the Process: Leading a Presidential Search in the Digital Age," *Trusteeship*, Nov.–Dec 2015, https://agb.org/trusteeship-article /the-pick-and-the-process-leading-a-presidential-search-in-the-digital-age/; Sydni Dunn, "More Public Colleges Opt for Closed Searches," *Chronicle of Higher Education*, June 3, 2013, https://www.chronicle.com/article/More-Public-Colleges-Opt-for /139569). In 2015, the American Association of University Professors (AAUP) made a statement denouncing secretive searches ("Statement on Presidential Searches," Association of Universities Professors, accessed on May 15, 2019, 2015, https://www .aaup.org/sites/default/fil/AAUP_Statement_on_Presidential_Searches_0.pdf). Open searches, however, can deter the strongest candidates, and many search firms advocate for balancing campus needs for inclusivity and candidates' needs for confidentiality (John Thornburgh, "Refining the Presidential Search Process," in *Best Practices in Higher Education Presidential Search*, (Witt/Kieffer, 2018), 6–8, https://www.wittkieffer.com/webfoo/wp-content/uploads/Best-Practices-in-Higher -Education-Presidential-Search_Witt-Kieffer_3rd-Edition.pdf).

13. The search firm Witt/Kiefer notes that "so much of the search process

cascades from this profile, and it should not be delegated to an ad hoc campus committee or left to a search consultant to cobble together a composite based on a series of interviews" (in *Best Practices in Higher Education Presidential Search* (Witt/ Kieffer, 2019), 7, https://www.wittkieffer.com/webfoo/wp-content/uploads/Best -Practices-in-Higher-Education-Presidential-Search_Witt-Kieffer_3rd-Edition.pdf).

14. Presidential profiles often emphasize specific characteristics, such as accountability, transparency, and humility (Oregon State University presidential profile, https://www.wittkieffer.com/position/president-7); identify explicit goals for the incoming president, such as maintaining a liberal arts–focused program for undergraduates and strengthening graduate program rankings ("An Invitation to Apply for the Position of President," Clark University, https://assets.storbeckpimen tel.com/files/resources/clark-president-pd.pdf?5d3607e3f117f); or express the need for candidates to be aligned with the intuitions' values and missions, including being committed to the school's faith, as in the case of private religious colleges (Presidential Leadership Profile, Saint Mary's College, https://www.saintmarys .edu/files/2019/07/19-285%20Leadership%20Profile%20ver%20208b.pdf).

15. There is a wide range of literature on the decision to become a president. See Harris, "Who Wants to Be a College President?"; Roger Martin, "So You Want to Become a College President?," RH Perry & Associates, https://rhperry.com/updates /so-you-want-to-become-a-college-president; Andy Thomason, "Is College President 'the Toughest Job in the Nation'?," *Chronicle of Higher Education*, May 1, 2018, https:// www.chronicle.com/article/Is-College-President-the/243289; Brian C. Mitchell, "Why Become a College President," *Huffington Post*, Feb. 16, 2014, https://www .huffpost.com/entry/college-president_b_4452587; Alan G. Merten, "So You Think You Want to Be a University President," Merten, American Council on Education, Spring 2012, https://www.acenet.edu/the-presidency/columns-and-features/Pages /So-You-Think-You-Want-to-Be-a-University-President.aspx.

16. For the past two-plus decades, college presidents have frequently been erroneously compared to CEOs; see, for example, Jeffrey J. Selingo, "Why College Presidents are Becoming More Like Corporate CEOs," *Washington Post*, Apr. 28, 2017, https://www.washingtonpost.com/news/grade-point/wp/2017/04/28/why -college-presidents-are-becoming-more-like-corporate-ceos/?noredirect=on&utm _term=.ea5030583a39; David Greenberg, "The College President as CEO," *Washington Post*, July 26, 1998, https://www.washingtonpost.com/archive/1998/07/26/the -college-president-as-ceo/3e18f9f4-7da2-4e7a-afc3-34a25a40daab/?utm_term= .6713bb238575.

17. For examples of why and how the president must have strong relationships with community stakeholders and leaders, including the governing officials, and the need to build these ties early in the presidency, see Nell Gluckman, "What Should a College President Do in Year One?," *Chronicle of Higher Education*, May 15, 2017, https://www.chronicle.com/article/What-Should-a-College/240074; Brian C. Mitchell, "Universities and the Public Good," *College Planning & Management*, July 1, 2013; Audrey Williams June, "Washington & Jefferson College, Once a Flashpoint

for Town-Gown Distrust, Offers a Model for Collaboration," *Chronicle of Higher Education*, Mar. 7, 2003, https://advance-lexis-com.ezproxy.library.wisc.edu/api/document?collection=news&id=urn:contentItem:489R-02X0-010P-J085-00000-00&context=1516831.

18. Joshua J. Yates and Michaela Accardi, *Field Guide for Urban University-Community Partnerships*, Institute for Advanced Studies in Culture (Charlottesville, VA, 2019), https://iasculture.org/research/publications/thriving-cities-field-guide; Julie Bourbon, "Partners in Progress: College, Community, and the Board's Contribution," *Trusteeship*, Jan.–Feb. 2015, https://agb.org/trusteeship-article/partners-in-progress-college-community-and-the-boards-contribution; Brian C. Mitchell and David Yeager, "Mending Fences," *College Planning & Management,* June 1, 2012. https://webcpm.com/articles/2012/06/01/mending-fences.aspx.

19. On the role of the president in annual giving, see Lawrence Biemiller, "Presidents of Small Colleges Bank on Fund Raising to Survive," *Chronicle of Higher Education*, Feb. 3, 2016, https://www.chronicle.com/article/Presidents-of-Small-Colleges/235148. Fundraising is becoming increasingly important at large public institutions as well (Lee Gardner, "Public Universities Are Getting Better at Bagging Big Gifts," *Chronicle of Higher Education*, Dec. 15, 2017, https://www-chronicle-com.ezproxy.library.wisc.edu/article/Public-Universities-Are/242072).

20. There are several annual leadership retreats and institutes geared toward cultivating this kind of network, including the American Association of State Colleges and Universities' Experienced Presidents Retreat and the Council of Independent Colleges' Presidents Institute.

21. Attention is increasingly being paid to the importance of emotional intelligence and empathy as critical qualities of the college president. A 2017 piece in the *Chronicle of Higher Education* on what search committees and governing boards should be looking for in presidents notes, "Emotional intelligence that enables leadership with empathy, respect, and cross-cultural competence is a must-have skill for aspiring higher-education leaders" (Robin Mamlet and Sheila Murphy, "6 Qualities to Look For in a College President," *Chronicle of Higher Education,* Sept. 17, 2017, https://advance-lexiscom.ezproxy.library.wisc.edu/api/document?collection=news&id=urn:contentItem:5PT5-8521-JCBF-K375-00000-00&context=1516831.) While another recent article states "emotional intelligence is especially important in higher education leadership because the culture of academe makes collaboration, reciprocity, and trust behavioral priorities. So emotional intelligence is a key component of the characteristics that we should seek in a college president" (Rita Bornstein, "The Missing Factor in Presidential Searches," *Trusteeship,* Jan.–Feb. 2015, https://agb.org/trusteeship-article/the-missing-factor-in-presidential-searches).

22. Jim Hunt, "5 Years Later: Jim Hunt Looks Back at Some Advice He Had for Fellow Provosts," *Inside Higher Ed*, July 18, 2014, https://www.insidehighered.com/advice/2014/07/18/essay-provost-reflects-advice-he-gave-new-provosts; Janel Curry, "The Education of a Provost," *Chronicle of Higher Education*, Dec. 18, 2012, https://www.chronicle.com/article/The-Education-of-a-Provost/136351.

23. Several recent studies and articles have noted that provosts do not neces-sarily aspire or transition to the presidencies, including the American Council on Education's Chief Academic Officer survey from 2013–14, which noted that 19% of the provosts surveyed became presidents (Chief Academic Officer Survey: CAO Professional Pathways, https://www.acenet.edu/news-room/Documents/Chief -Academic-Officer-Survey-CAO-Professional-Pathways.pdf). See also Harris, "Who Wants to Be a College President?"; Jeffrey Selingo, Sonny Chheng, and Cole Clark, "Pathways to the university presidency: The future of higher education leadership," Deloitte Insights, 2017, https://www2.deloitte.com/insights/us/en/industry/public -sector/college-presidency-higher-education-leadership.html; Paul Fain, "Why Do Few Provosts Want to Be Presidents? Survey Suggests Some Answers," *Chronicle of Higher Education*, July 20, 2010, https://www.chronicle.com/article/Why-Do-Few -Provosts-Want-to-Be/123614.

24. There is a large literature on these partnerships; see, for example, Mitchell A. Levy and Bernard A. Polnariev, eds., *Academic And Student Affairs in Collabora-tion: Creating a Culture of Student Success* (New York: Routledge, 2016); Adrianna Kezar, Deborah J. Hirsch, and Cathy Burack, eds., *Understanding the Role of Academic and Student Affairs Collaboration in Creating a Successful Learning Environment* (San Francisco: Jossey-Bass, 2002).

25. Neil Swidey, "Our College Sports System Is Broken," *Boston Globe Magazine*, May 15, 2019, https://www.bostonglobe.com/magazine/2019/05/15/our-college -sports-system-broken-have-guts-fix/sI2mfTpEUlAZqRUS5VAr6J/story.html; Kirk Carapezza, "Change Still Tricky as Sentencing in Varsity Blues Scandal Begins," WGBH News, June 12, 2019, https://www.wgbh.org/news/education/2019/06/12 /change-still-tricky-as-sentencing-in-varsity-blues-scandal-begins; Brad Wolver-ton, "How Athletics and Academics Collided at One University," *Chronicle of Higher Education*, June 10, 2015 https://advance-lexis-com.ezproxy.library.wisc.edu/api /document?collection=news&id=urn:contentItem:5G8V-RCJ1-DYTH-9002-00000 -00&context=1516831; Therese A. McCarty, "Athletics and Academics Can Be a Winning Partnership," *Chronicle of Higher Education*, May 12, 2014, https://advance -lexis-com.ezproxy.library.wisc.edu/api/document?collection=news&id=urn:content Item:5C6P-M6J1-JCBF-K00M-00000-00&context=1516831.

26. Plentiful resources exist on how to be an effective and adept board chair and board member: Association of Governing Boards of Universities and Colleges (AGB), *Overseeing Educational Quality: A How-To Guide for Boards of Universities and Colleges* (Washington, DC: Association of Governing Boards of Universities and Colleges, 2014), https://agb.org/reports-and-statements/overseeing-educational -quality-a-how-to-guide-for-boards-of-universities-and-collegesl; Robert Scott, *How University Boards Work: A Guide for Trustees, Officers, and Leaders in Higher Education* (Baltimore: Johns Hopkins University Press, 2018); Stephen R. Lewis Jr., "What I Wanted, and Got, from my Board Chairs," last modified Aug. 17, 2017, https://apps.carleton.edu/campus/president/slewis/speeches_writings/board_chairs/; Jeffrey B. Trammel, *Effective Board Chairs: A Guide for University and College Chairs*

(Washington, DC: Association of Governing Boards of Universities and Colleges, 2016); "The Four Cs of Board Leadership," *Trusteeship*, Sep.–Oct. 2016, https://agb .org/trusteeship-article/the-four-cs-of-board-leadership/.

27. The Association of Governing Boards offers a wealth of resources, including Scott D. Miller, "Getting on Board: How Presidents and Trustees Can Build Successful Strategies," *Trusteeship*, May–June 2017, https://agb.org/trusteeship-article /getting-on-board-how-presidents-and-trustees-can-build-successful-strategies; "The President–Board Chair Relationship: Making It Work, Making It Count," *Trusteeship*, Nov.–Dec. 2014, https://agb.org/trusteeship-article/the-president-board -chair-relationship-making-it-work-making-it-count; Peter Eckel, "What Presidents Really Think about Their Boards," *Trusteeship*, Nov.–Dec. 2013.

28. E. B. Wilson, "Creating a Cadre of Leaders on College and University Boards," *Trusteeship*, Mar.–Apr. 2015, https://agb.org/trusteeship-article/creating -a-cadre-of-leaders-on-college-and-university-boards.

29. Brian C. Mitchell, "The New Rules of Engagement," *Academe*, May–June 2013, https://www.aaup.org/article/new-rules-engagement#.XTXmBXt7ncs; Trammel, *Effective Board Chairs: A Guide for University and College Chairs*.

Chapter 2. Strategic Planning

1. "Strategy, n." *OED Online* (Oxford University Press, 2019), https://www-oed -com.ezproxy.library.wisc.edu/view/Entry/191319?rskey=70DRdQ&result=1&is Advanced=false.

2. Roger L. Martin, "Don't Let Strategy Become Planning," *Harvard Business Review*, Feb. 5, 2013, https://hbr.org/2013/02/dont-let-strategy-become-plann.

3. Susan Resneck Pierce, "Hope and Denial Are Not Strategies," *Inside Higher Ed*, Jan. 31, 2017, https://www.insidehighered.com/views/2017/01/31/how-colleges -should-rethink-their-strategic-planning-processes-essay.

4. Carl von Clausewitz, *On War*, ed. and trans. Michael Howard and Peter Paret (Princeton, NJ: Princeton University Press, 1976), 617.

5. Martin, "Don't Let Strategy Become Planning."

6. Clausewitz, *On War*, 132.

7. This Latin aphorism is found in Francis Bacon's *Meditationes Sacrae* (London: Excusum impensis Humfredi Hooper, 1597).

8. James C. Collins, *Built to Last: Successful Habits of Visionary Companies* (New York: Harper Business, 1994).

9. Karen E. Hinton, *A Practical Guide to Strategic Planning in Higher Education* (Johnstown, NY: Society for College and University Planning, 2012); "Game Plan: New Directions in Strategic Thinking and Planning," *Trusteeship*, Nov.–Dec. 2017, https://agb.org/trusteeship-article/game-plan-new-directions-in-strategic-thinking -and-planning/; John M. Bryson, *Strategic Planning for Public and Nonprofit Organizations* (Hoboken, NJ: John Wiley & Sons, 2018).

10. Allison Task, "Anyone Can Innovate Like Walt Disney by Following His

Simple Process," *Entrepreneur*, July 18, 2018, https://www.entrepreneur.com /article/316144.

11. The concept of six thinking hats (Edward de Bono, *Six Thinking Hats* [Boston: Little, Brown, 1985]) is summarized by the de Bono Group: http://www .debonogroup.com/six_thinking_hats.php.

12. "IDEO, Design Thinking" (website), accessed Aug. 19, 2019, https://design thinking.ideo.com.

13. Eugene M. Tobin, "The Future of Liberal Arts Colleges Begins with Collaboration," in *Remaking College: Innovation and the Liberal Arts College*, ed. Rebecca Chopp, Susan Frost, and Daniel H. Weiss (Baltimore: Johns Hopkins University Press, 2013), 129.

14. "AQIP Pathway Overview," Higher Learning Commission, accessed Aug. 19, 2019, https://www.hlcommission.org/Accreditation/aqip-overview.html.

15. Southern Association of Colleges and Schools Commission on Colleges, "The Quality Enhancement Plan," last updated June 2018, http://www.sacscoc.org /pdf/081705/Quality%20Enhancement%20Plan.pdf.

16. Louis Brandeis, *Other People's Money and How the Bankers Use It* (New York: F. A. Stokes, 1914), 92.

17. "Campus Master Plan," Virginia Tech (website), accessed Aug. 19, 2019, https://www.facilities.vt.edu/planning-construction/campus-master-plan.html

18. Ibid.

19. "From Thomas Jefferson to Joseph Priestley, 18 January 1800," *Founders Online*, National Archives, accessed Apr. 11, 2019, https://founders.archives.gov /documents/Jefferson/01-31-02-0275.

20. "From Thomas Jefferson to Littleton W. Tazewell, 5 January 1805," *Founders Online*, National Archives, accessed Apr. 11, 2019, https://founders.archives.gov /documents/Jefferson/99-01-02-0958.

21. "Thomas Jefferson to the Trustees of the Lottery for East Tennessee College, 6 May 1810," *Founders Online*, National Archives, accessed Apr. 11, 2019, https:// founders.archives.gov/documents/Jefferson/03-02-02-0322.

22. Whitman College, "Diversity Innovation Grants" (website), accessed Nov. 10, 2020, https://www.whitman.edu/campus-life/diversity/diversity-innovation -grants.

Chapter 3. Management and Operations

1. Eric Hoover, "'Act Now!' Say Hello to the New Enrollment Playbook," *Chronicle of Higher Education*, Feb. 11, 2020, https://www.chronicle.com/article/Act-Now -Say-Hello-to/248030.

2. Dana Goldstein, "Cheating Scandals, Charters and Falling Test Scores: 5 takeaways from the year in education," *New York Times*, Dec. 27, 2019, https://www .nytimes.com/2019/12/27/us/cheating-scandals-charters-and-falling-test-scores-5 -takeaways-from-the-year-in-education.html.

3. Hoover, "Act Now! Say Hello to the New Enrollment Playbook."

4. Ibid.

5. EAB, *Enrollment Strategy after the NACAC Vote* (Washington, DC: EAB, 2020).

6. Ibid., 5.

7. Scott Jaschik and Doug Lederman, eds., *2019 Survey of College and University Admissions Officials* (Washington, DC: Inside Higher Ed, 2019).

8. Ibid.

9. Angel B. Perez, "What Is a Chief Enrollment Officer?," *Inside Higher Ed*, Aug. 12, 2019, https://www.insidehighered.com/admissions/views/2019/08/12/defining -role-chief-enrollment-officer-important-opinion.

10. Ibid.

11. "Capital Campaigns," *Inside Higher Ed*, https://www.insidehighered.com /capital_campaigns.

12. "Why Does College Feel Out of Reach for Too Many?," St. John's College (website), https://freeingminds.sjc.edu/the-problem/.

13. Ibid.

14. "How Do We Help More Students Access Education?," St. John's College (website), https://freeingminds.sjc.edu/our-solution/.

15. "Gordon College Unveils a $130 Million 'Faith Rising' Campaign to Serve Future Students," *The Bell: News and Stories from Gordon College*, Oct. 4, 2019, http://stories.gordon.edu/gordon-college-unveils-a-130-million-faith-rising -campaign-to-serve-future-students/.

16. Dan Allenby, "Class Exodus," *CASE Currents*, Oct. 2014, 26.

17. Anna Corradi and Matt Schifrin, "Grateful Grads 2019: Follow Alumni Love and Money into the Best Colleges," *Forbes*, Aug. 15, 2019, https://www.forbes.com /sites/annacorradi/2019/08/15/grateful-grads-2019-follow-alumni-love-and-money -into-the-best-colleges/#43ac78e66ca2.

18. Sue Cunningham, "Rankings Must Reconsider Alumni Giving Rates," *Inside Higher Ed*, Sept. 17, 2018, https://www.insidehighered.com/views/2018/09/17/us -news-rankings-provide-profoundly-limited-view-alumni-relations-opinion.

19. (https://www.insidehighered.com/news/2019/06/20/donations-colleges-are -number-donors-down).

20. Jaschik and Lederman, *2019 Survey of College and University Business Officers*.

21. Ibid.

22. Thomas Ayers and Karen Goldstein, "Becoming a Renaissance CBO," *Inside Higher Ed*, June 5, 2015, https://www.insidehighered.com/advice/2015/06/05/chief -business-officers-must-broaden-their-skills-and-roles-essay.

23. Kasia Moreno, "The Renaissance CFO," *Forbes*, Dec.14, 2015, https://www .forbes.com/sites/forbesinsights/2015/12/14/the-renaissance-cfo/#57840b60e8d2 https://www.forbes.com/sites/forbesinsights/2015/12/14/the-renaissance-cfo /#57840b60e8d2.

24. Don Mailliard, "The Rise of the Renaissance CFO," *Insights*, June 6, 2016,

https://home.kpmg/xx/en/home/insights/2016/06/the-rise-of-the-renaissance-cfo
.html.

25. Ibid.

26. Aaron Benz to Joseph King, personal communication, Jan. 22, 2020.

27. Aaron Benz, "Why We Exist," Degree Analytics (website), Dec. 6, 2017,
https://degreeanalytics.com/news/why-we-exist/.

28. Michael S. Harris and Molly K. Ellis, "Exploring Involuntary Presidential
Turnover in American Higher Education," *Journal of Higher Education* 89, no. 3
(2018): 294–317.

29. Ibid.

30. Laura McKenna, "Why Are Fewer College Presidents Academics?," *The
Atlantic*, Dec.3. 2015, https://www.theatlantic.com/education/archive/2015/12/college
-president-mizzou-tim-wolfe/418599/.

31. Stephen Ambrose, *Eisenhower: Soldier, General of the Army, President-Elect
(1893–1952)* (New York: Simon & Schuster, 1983).

32. Sean Michael Heuvel, "Culture Clash: A Case Study of the Issues that Nontraditional College Presidents Face in Adjusting to Academic Culture" (PhD diss.,
William & Mary, 2015), 173.

33. Jack Quinan, *Frank Lloyd Wright's Larkin Building* (Chicago: University of
Chicago Press, 2006), 99.

34. Ibid., 137.

35. Beckie Supiano, "U. of Tulsa Has a Billion-Dollar Endowment for Just 4,000
Students: Why Is It Cutting Programs?," *Chronicle of Higher Education*, Apr. 15, 2019,
https://www.chronicle.com/article/U-of-Tulsa-Has-a/246117.

36. Ibid.

37. Ibid.

38. Randy Krehbiel, "TU Faculty Votes 'No Confidence' in President Gerard
Clancy, Provost Janet Levit," *Tulsa World*, Nov. 14, 2019, https://www.tulsaworld
.com/news/local/education/tu-faculty-votes-no-confidence-in-president-gerard
-clancy-provost-janet-levit/article_5d5842ec-0335-504f-aaad-ef557e84363e.html.

39. Ibid.

40. Gary A. Olson, "Why Universities Reorganize," *Chronicle of Higher Education*, Aug. 15, 2010, https://www.chronicle.com/article/Why-Universities-Reorganize
/123903.

41. Ibid.

42. "University of Mary Elects young High School Religion Teacher as President,"
Catholic New Agency (website), Dec 11, 2008, https://www.catholicnewsagency
.com/news/university_of_mary_elects_young_high_school_religion_teacher_as
_president.

43. "University of Mary Campaign Will Reshape Campus and Enrich Our
Students," University of Mary (website), Oct. 19, 2015, https://news.umary.edu
/university-of-mary-campaign-will-reshape-campus-and-enrich-our-students/.

44. Ibid.

45. "University of Mary Eclipses $100-Million Mark, Surpasses Goal and Closes Phase-I of Vision 2030 Capital Campaign," University of Mary (website), Feb.12, 2019, https://news.umary.edu/university-of-mary-eclipses-100-million-mark-surpasses-goal-and-closes-phase-i-of-vision-2030-capital-campaign/.

46. Brian C. Mitchell and W. Joseph King, *How to Run a College: A Practical Guide for Trustees, Faculty, Administrators, and Policymakers* (Baltimore: Johns Hopkins University Press, 2018), 77.

47. Nick Hazelrigg, "For Liberal Arts College Woes, an Answer in Smaller Boards?," *Inside Higher Ed*, Aug. 2, 2019, https://www.insidehighered.com/news/2019/08/02/size-reduction-lyon-college-board-allows-college-better-respond-problems.

48. Ibid.

49. Thomas Paine, *The American Crisis*, American Memory Timeline, Library of Congress, http://www.loc.gov/teachers/classroommaterials/presentationsand activities/presentations/timeline/amrev/north/paine.html.

Chapter 4. Stakeholder Relations

1. In response to concern that faculty, generally, does not have explicit training in governance and leadership, David D. Perlmutter has authored a series of columns for the *Chronicle of Higher Education* called "Administration 101;" see, e.g., "Deciding to Lead: Are You Prepared for the Types, Scale, and Severity of Management Challenges?," *Chronicle of Higher Education*, Jan. 1, 2017, https://www.chronicle.com/article/Administration-101-Deciding/238757.

2. E. B. Wilson, "Creating a Cadre of Leaders on College and University Boards," *Trusteeship*, Mar.–Apr. 2015, http://agb.org/trusteeship/2015/marchapril/creating-a-cadre-of-leaders-on-college-and-university-boards.

3. Several examples of presidents who failed in part due to unpreparedness are detailed in Stephen Joel Trachtenberg, Gerald B. Kauvar, and E. Grady Bogue, *Presidencies Derailed: Why University Leaders Fail and How to Prevent It* (Baltimore: Johns Hopkins University Press, 2013).

4. Training and advising resources for new presidents include: The AGB Institute for Leadership & Governance in Higher Education, and the Harvard Seminar for New Presidents.

5. As noted, search committees often provide consultants whom presidents might continue to rely on through their first year. Some presidential training groups, like the New President's program at Harvard, have trusted mentors, who can be valuable seasoned colleagues with informed opinions. Presidential associations at the state level and faith-based groups often have presidents and executive directors who provided continued insight.

6. The *Chronicle* recently published a piece by a former academic search firm associate on the merits of closed searches (Matthew Tzuker, "Sorry, Professors, but Presidential Searches Should Be Secret," *Chronicle of Higher Education*, June 3, 2019, https://www.chronicle.com/article/Sorry-Professors-but/246424), which prompted

a response by a faculty member and board chair at Pomona State (Kevin Dettmar and Sam Glick, "Sorry, Headhunters, but the Healthiest Presidential Searches Are Open," *Chronicle of Higher Education*, July 2, 2019, https://www.chronicle.com /article/Sorry-Headhunters-but-the/246597). See also Nick Hazelrigg, "Secret Searches and Faculty Fury," *Inside Higher Ed*, Aug. 23, 2019, https://www.inside highered.com/news/2019/08/23/faculty-anger-surrounding-several-presidential -searches-some-point-search-firms.

7. There is a wealth of resources on how campuses can best prepare for leadership transitions, including Scott D. Miller and Marylouise Fennell, "Presidential Transitions," *College Planning & Management*, Apr. 1, 2016, https://webcpm.com /Articles/2016/04/01/New-CEO.aspx; Kina Mallard, David W. Miles, and Larry Zimpleman, "Inaugural Transitions: Providing the Start That All Presidents and Institutions Deserve," *Trusteeship*, Nov.–Dec. 2015, https://agb.org/trusteeship -article/inaugural-transitions; Theodore Marchese, "Making the Most of Presidential Transitions," *Trusteeship*, Jan.–Feb. 2012, https://agb.org/trusteeship-article /making-the-most-of-presidential-transitions/; Gwendolyn Evans Jensen and Lorna Duphiney Edmundson, "The Ten Commandments of Presidential Transition," *Chronicle of Higher Education*, Feb. 26, 2002, https://www.chronicle.com/article /The-Ten-Commandments-of/46254.

8. In the American Council on Education's *2016 American College President Study*, 35 percent of respondents reported being frustrated by the problems inherited from the previous leadership. Examples include Audrey Williams June, "Combatants Become Allies," *Chronicle of Higher Education*, Mar. 7, 2003, https:// www.chronicle.com/article/Combatants-Become-Allies/35994.

9. Jake B. Schrum, "Evaluating Presidential Candidates," *Change: The Magazine of Higher Learning* (July–Aug. 2013), 24–25.

10. Sarah C. Mangelsdorf, "A message from President Mangelsdorf," last modified July 1, 2019, https://www.rochester.edu/president; Scott D. Miller, "Surviving a Presidential Transition," *Inside Higher Ed*, Feb. 10, 2016.

11. There are many recent historical cases of tense relationships between presidents and board chairs. For example, Margaret Spellings, the former president of the UNC system, experienced high-profile tensions with the board (Joe Killian, "Trove of Emails Provides a Window into Conflicts at UNC," NC Policy Watch, Jan. 2018, http://www.ncpolicywatch.com/2018/01/10/trove-emails-provides-window -conflicts-unc), while Janice Cervelli, the former president of St. Mary's College, sued the institution, claiming that she was forced out by the chair of the board of trustees (Greg Toppo, "President Sues College over Departure, Pay," *Inside Higher Ed*, Mar. 15, 2019, https://www.insidehighered.com/news/2019/03/15/dismissed -president-sues-saint-mary%E2%80%99s-college-indiana).

12. Joye Mercer, "Yale Returns a $20-Million Gift," *Chronicle of Higher Education*, Mar. 24, 1995, https://www.chronicle.com/article/Yale-Returns-a-20-Million/83682; Jennifer Kaylin, "Bass, Yale, and Western Civ.," *Yale Alumni Magazine*, Summer 1995, http://archives.yalealumnimagazine.com/issues/95_07/bass.html. There are

other, more recent and prominent examples of major gifts being returned to donors, including the University of Alabama Law School returning a $26.5-million gift to Hugh F. Culverhouse Jr. over his outspoken prochoice stance on abortion, and Cornell declining a gift from architect Richard Meier after sexual misconduct charges arose against him (Richard Fausset, "University of Alabama Returns Largest-Ever Gift to Donor," *New York Times*, June 7, 2019, https://www.nytimes.com/2019/06/07/us/alabama-university-culverhouse-donation.html; Scott Jaschik, "Why Alabama Returned the Gift," *Inside Higher Ed*, June 10, 2019, https://www.insidehighered.com/news/2019/06/10/why-did-university-alabama-return-millions-donor), Rick Seltzer, "Cornell Returns Gift after Misconduct Charges against Donor," *Inside Higher Ed*, Mar. 15, 2018, https://www.insidehighered.com/quicktakes/2018/03/15/cornell-returns-gift-after-misconduct-charges-against-donor).

13. Susan Resneck Pierce, "Talking Presidents off the Ledge," *Inside Higher Ed*, Apr. 24, 2018, https://www.insidehighered.com/views/2018/04/24/how-presidents-today-must-deal-problems-they-didnt-create-and-cant-control-opinion. The *Chronicle of Higher Education* launched a video series, "On Leadership," in which college presidents and top administrators discuss many examples of crisis leadership (https://www.chronicle.com/specialreport/On-Leadership/29). The Council for Advancement and Support of Education (CASE) has a resource collection for members on how to develop crisis management plans and communications strategies: https://www.case.org/resources/subject-guide-crisis-planning-management.

14. "College Presidents on Social Media: A 2018 Snapshot," BriefCASE, Apr. 1, 2018, https://www.case.org/trending/college-presidents-social-media-2018-snapshot; Lindsay McKenzie, "A College President's Twitter Strategy," *Inside Higher Ed*, June 15, 2018, https://www.insidehighered.com/news/2018/06/15/drawing-line-between-policy-and-personality-twitter; Dan Zaiontz, *#FollowTheLeader: Lessons in Social Media Success from #HigherEd CEOs* (Saint Louis, MO: EDUniverse Media, 2015); Marybeth Gasman, "HBCU Presidents and Social Media," *Huffington Post*, Nov. 5, 2012, https://www.huffpost.com/entry/hbcu-social-media-use_b_1856214; "The Big Picture: Conversations with College Presidents on Branding and Higher Education," *Peer to Peer*, vol. 3; http://ologie.com/wp-content/uploads/2016/06/OLM-074-P2P3_Magazine_v9_PRO-1.pdf.

15. There are training and professional development opportunities available on the role of presidents and fundraising, including the sessions at the CIC's Presidents Institute, or the more focused "Fundraising for Presidents Institute," run by Academic Impressions. https://www.academicimpressions.com/fundraising-presidents-institute.

16. Benjamin Ginsberg, "The Strategic Plan: Neither Strategy nor Plan, but a Waste of Time," *Chronicle of Higher Education*, July 17, 2011, https://www.chronicle.com/article/The-Strategic-Plan-Neither/128227. Colleges risk losing accreditation when they refuse to partake in strategic planning. For example, Wilberforce University was put on probation by the Higher Learning Commission in 2018 (Max Filby, "Wilberforce U. Placed on Probation for Failing to Meet Accreditation Standards,"

Dayton Daily News, Aug. 9, 2018, https://www.daytondailynews.com/news/wilber
force-placed-probation-for-failing-meet-accreditation-standards/CquP6aSb6PLYp
MjMYv1WpL.

17. Tara M. Samuels, "Listening to the Wrong People" *Inside Higher Ed*, Apr.
14, 2014, https://www.insidehighered.com/advice/2014/04/14/essay-new-college
-presidents-who-get-their-advice-wrong-people.

18. Most provosts were faculty members or deans in their prior positions
(Audrey Williams June and Dan Bauman, "The Provost's Path," *Chronicle of Higher
Education*, Jan. 13, 2019, https://www.chronicle.com/interactives/provost). For a
curated list of advice articles for faculty seeking leadership positions, see the
Chronicle of Higher Education's special report "How Do I Become an Administra-
tor?," (https://www.chronicle.com/specialreport/How-Do-I-Become-an/80?cid
=RCPACKAGE); see also George Justice and Carolyn Dever, "Beyond the Dark
Side," *Inside Higher Ed*, May 16, 2019, https://www.insidehighered.com/advice/2019
/05/16/practical-advice-faculty-members-considering-joining-administration
-opinion.

19. A 2018 report from the American Council on Education includes discussion
on the importance of developing and maintaining a senior team (Louis Soares,
Jonathan S. Gagliardi, Philip J. Wilkinson, et al., *Innovative Leadership: Insights from
the American College President Study 2017* [Washington, DC: American Council on
Education, 2018]). Recent articles also explore the role of senior staff: Pat Sanaghan,
"Dismantling the Senior Team: A Troubling Trend," *Inside Higher Ed*, June 6, 2019,
https://www.insidehighered.com/advice/2019/06/06/why-new-presidents-shouldnt
-dismantle-current-senior-team-opinion; Katherine Haley, "Team of Rivals," *Inside
Higher Ed*, July 17, 2019, https://www.insidehighered.com/advice/2019/07/17/why
-and-how-boards-must-help-new-presidents-manage-their-senior-teams-opinion.

20. Michael T. Marsden, "What Makes a Good Chief Academic Officer?," *Inside
Higher Ed*, Nov.15, 2018, https://www.insidehighered.com/advice/2018/11/15/guidance
-chief-academic-officers-liberal-arts-colleges-opinion; James Martin, *The Provost's
Handbook* (Baltimore: Johns Hopkins University Press, 2015); Janel Curry, "The
Education of a Provost," *Chronicle of Higher Education*, Dec. 18, 2012, https://www
.chronicle.com/article/The-Education-of-a-Provost/136351.

21. Michael Bugeja, "What Do Provosts and Deans Actually Do?," *Inside Higher
Ed*, Feb. 14, 2018, https://www.insidehighered.com/views/2018/02/14/poorly-defined
-roles-provosts-and-deans-can-lead-problems-major-universities; Ray Maghroori
and Charles Powers, "Vice President vs. Provost," *Chronicle of Higher Education*,
Aug. 2, 2007, https://www.chronicle.com/article/Vice-President-vs-Provost/46483.

22. American Council on Education, Chief Academic Officer Survey: CAO
Professional Pathways, https://www.acenet.edu/news-room/Documents/Chief
-Academic-Officer-Survey-CAO-Professional-Pathways.pdf. See also Adam Harris,
"Who Wants to Be a College President?," *The Atlantic*, Jan. 24, 2019; Jeffrey Selingo,
Sonny Chheng, Cole Clark, "Pathways to the University Presidency: The Future of
Higher Education Leadership," Deloitte Insights, 2017, https://www2.deloitte.com

/insights/us/en/industry/public-sector/college-presidency-higher-education-leadership.html; Paul Fain, "Why Do Few Provosts Want to Be Presidents? Survey Suggests Some Answers," *Chronicle of Higher Education*, July 20, 2010, https://www.chronicle.com/article/Why-Do-Few-Provosts-Want-to-Be/123614.

23. Harold V. Hartley III and Eric E. Godin, *A Study of Chief Academic Officers of Independent Colleges and Universities* (Washington, DC: Council of Independent Colleges, 2010).

24. As noted in chapter 1, college presidents typically spend seven years in the position, according to the *The American College President, 2017*, study, while the *Chronicle* found that the average tenure for provosts is approximately five years (June and Bauman, "The Provost's Path"). Michael S. Harris and Molly K. Ellis founds that the vast majority of involuntary turnover in college presidencies occurs before the fifth year of tenure ("Exploring Involuntary Presidential Turnover in American Higher Education," *Journal of Higher Education* 89, no. 3 (2018): 294–317. John Engler recently became the second president to leave Michigan State University in one year (https://www.theatlantic.com/education/archive/2019/01/engler-resigns-michigan-state-interim-president-udpa/580699/).

25. Nick Hazelrigg, "For Liberal Arts College Woes, an Answer in Smaller Boards?," *Inside Higher Ed*, Aug. 2, 2019, http://www.insidehighered.com/news/2019/08/02/size-reduction-lyon-college-board-allows-college-better-respond-problems; Jack Stripling, "Too Many Trustees Can Burden a Board, More Colleges Realize," *Chronicle of Higher Education*, Aug. 13, 2012, https://www.chronicle.com/article/Shrink-My-Board-Please/133557; Brian C. Mitchell and W. Joseph King, *How to Run a College: A Practical Guide for Trustees, Faculty, Administrators, and Policymakers* (Baltimore: Johns Hopkins University Press, 2018), 1.

26. Steven C. Bahls, "How to Make Shared Governance Work: Some Best Practices," *Trusteeship*, Mar.–Apr. 2014, https://agb.org/trusteeship-article/how-to-make-shared-governance-work-some-best-practices.

27. Many institutions have created offices dedicated to parent relations, including Bradley University (Alan Galsky and Joyce Shotick, "Managing Millennial Parents," *Chronicle of Higher Education*, Jan. 5, 2012, https://www.chronicle.com/article/Managing-Millennial-Parents/130146/). The author (Mitchell) describes the role of parents in "The Rules of the Game in College Governance," *Huffington Post*, Aug. 24, 2016, https://www.huffpost.com/entry/the-rules-of-the-game-in_b_8031312.

28. James O. Freedman noted that alumni, while often loyal, "can also be indifferent to an institution's shortcomings and unduly resistant to proposals that threaten to alter its familiar character," in Ronald G. Ehrenberg, ed., *Governing Academia: Who Is in Charge at the Modern University?* (Ithaca, NY: Cornell University Press, 2015), 12; Paul Fain, "Governing Boards Should Look beyond Alumni for Trustees, Report Says," *Chronicle of Higher Education*, Apr. 29, 2010, https://www.chronicle.com/article/Governing-Boards-Should-Look/65325.

Chapter 5. Campus and Community

1. Blake Gumprecht, *The American College Town* (Amherst: University of Massachusetts Press, 2008); Joshua Kim, "Small Town College Life and the Future of Higher Ed," *Inside Higher Ed*, Oct. 31, 2016, https://www.insidehighered.com/blogs /technology-and-learning/small-town-college-life-and-future-higher-ed; Witold Rybczynski, "The Best Places to Live in America. How College Towns Perfected the City," *Salon*, Sept. 20, 2015, https://www.salon.com/2015/09/19/the_best_places _to_live_in_america_how_college_towns_perfected_the_city; Alana Semuels, "Could Small-Town Harvards Revive Rural Economies?," *The Atlantic*, May 2, 2017, https://www.theatlantic.com/business/archive/2017/05/rural-economies-colleges -development/525114.

2. Cara Newlon, "The College Amenities Arms Race," *Forbes*, July 31, 2014, https://www.forbes.com/sites/caranewlon/2014/07/31/the-college-amenities-arms -race/#750754764883; Jeffrey Selingo, "Why Universities Are Phasing Out Luxury Dorms," *The Atlantic*, Aug. 21, 2017, https://www.theatlantic.com/education/archive /2017/08/why-universities-are-phasing-out-luxury-dorms/537492/; Kellie Woodhouse, "Lazy Rivers and Student Debt," *Inside Higher Ed*, June 15, 2015, https:// www.insidehighered.com/news/2015/06/15/are-lazy-rivers-and-climbing-walls -driving-cost-college; Dawn Wotapka, "Resort Living Comes to Campus," *Wall Street Journal*, Dec. 6, 2012, https://www.wsj.com/articles/SB1000142412788732 3830404578145591134362564.

3. Town/gown tension is as old as the university itself (Laurence Brockliss, "Gown and Town: The University and the City in Europe, 1200–2000," *Minerva* 38, no. 2 (2000): 147–70), but recent examples abound, including Josh Keller, "California Confronts Town-Gown Rifts," *Chronicle of Higher Education*, June 8, 2007, https://www.chronicle.com/article/California-Confronts-Town-Gown/26993; Scott Jaschik, "Town-Gown Dispute and New Law in Rhode Island," *Inside Higher Ed*, July 12, 2013, https://www.insidehighered.com/quicktakes/2013/07/12/town-gown -dispute-and-new-law-rhode-island; Mike DeBonis, "Seeking Balance in D.C.'s Town-Gown Relations," *Washington Post*, Oct. 26, 2011, https://www.washington post.com/blogs/mike-debonis/post/seeking-balance-in-dcs-town-gown-relations /2011/10/26/gIQAcg98IM_blog.html; Amy Scott, "There Goes the Neighborhood: The College Students Next Door," Marketplace (website), Sept. 22, 2014, https:// www.marketplace.org/2014/09/22/there-goes-neighborhood-college-students-next -door/

4. Timothy Bartik and George Erickcek, "The Local Economic Impact of "Eds & Meds": How Policies to Expand Universities and Hospitals Affect Metropolitan Economies," Brookings Institution, Dec. 2008, https://www.brookings.edu/research /the-local-economic-impact-of-eds-meds-how-policies-to-expand-universities-and -hospitals-affect-metropolitan-economies; Brian C. Mitchell and W. Joseph King, "Boston is the Nation's College Capital," *Boston Globe Magazine*, Apr. 3, 2018, https://

www.bostonglobe.com/magazine/2018/04/03/boston-nation-college-capital-here
-how-keep-that-way/1OINDOWirlTaCHrcszctGK/story.html; Kim Hart, "College
Towns Are Becoming Economic Powerhouses," *Axios*, Sept. 4, 2019, https://www
.axios.com/college-towns-emerge-as-economic-powerhouses-7065b754-3889-46fb
-82c2-5aadb1ed6398.html.

5. John C. Austin, "Tale of Two Rust Belts: Diverging Economic Paths Shaping
Community Politics," *The Avenue*, Brookings Institution, June 30, 2017, https://
www.brookings.edu/blog/the-avenue/2017/06/30/a-tale-of-two-rust-belts-diverging
-economic-paths-shaping-community-politics.

6. Recent media coverage of this issue includes Alia Wong, "The Surreal End
of an American College," *The Atlantic*, June 18, 2019, https://www.theatlantic.com
/education/archive/2019/06/what-its-like-when-your-college-shuts-down/591862/;
Michael Vasquez and Dan Bauman, "How America's College-Closure Crisis Leaves
Families Devastated," *Chronicle of Higher Education*, Apr. 4, 2019, https://www
.chronicle.com/interactives/20190404-ForProfit; Elizabeth Hewitt, "The Other
Victims When Colleges Decline or Close: Their Hometowns," *Hechinger Report*,
Feb. 12, 2019, https://hechingerreport.org/the-other-victims-when-colleges-decline
-or-close-their-hometowns; Jon Kamp, "In Vermont, Small Colleges Are Closing,"
Wall Street Journal, May 17, 2019, https://www.wsj.com/articles/in-vermont-small
-colleges-are-closing-11558092600

7. Brian C. Mitchell, "Local Community Hit Hard When College Closes," *Huffington Post*, Feb. 13, 2017, https://www.huffpost.com/entry/local-community-hit
-hard_b_14721692

8. Meredith Colias, "Rensselaer Stunned after Announcement of St. Joseph's
Closure," *Chicago Tribune*, Feb. 10, 2017, https://www.chicagotribune.com/suburbs
/post-tribune/ct-ptb-rensselaer-st-joseph-closure-st-0212-20170210-story.html.

9. Ibid.

10. Audrey Williams June, "How Community Service Can Help Your Career,"
Chronicle of Higher Education, July 17, 2017, https://www.chronicle.com/article/How
-Community-Service-Can-Help/240622; David M. Perry, "But Does It Count?,"
Chronicle of Higher Education, June 23, 2014, https://www.chronicle.com/article
/But-Does-It-Count-/147199.

11. Scott Carlson, *The Campus as City: Crucial Strategies to Bolster Town-Gown
Relations and Run a Thriving 21st-Century Institution* (Washington, DC: Chronicle
of Higher Education, 2019); Lawrence V. Weill, "The President's Role in Cultivating
Positive Town-Gown Relations," *Planning for Higher Education* 37, no. 4. (2009):
37–42; Hannah Chenoweth, "How Can Universities Strengthen Town-Gown Relations?," *Higher Ed Facilities Forum*, Dec. 6, 2017, https://info.higheredfacilitiesforum
.com/blog/how-universities-can-strengthen-town-gown-relations.

12. Brian C. Mitchell and Lee Fritschler, "A Taxing Situation," *Trusteeship*,
Sept.–Oct. 1995, 12–17; Patrick Healy, "Pa. Court Voids Ban on Private College's Tax
Exemptions," *Chronicle of Higher Education*, Sept. 29, 1995, https://www.chronicle
.com/article/Pa-Court-Voids-Ban-on-Private/95739; Brian C. Mitchell, "Private

Colleges Should Stay on Guard against Challenges to Their Tax-Exempt Status," *Chronicle of Higher Education*, Dec. 12, 1997, https://www.chronicle.com/article /Private-Colleges-Should-Stay/97676.

13. Audrey Williams June, "Combatants Become Allies," *Chronicle of Higher Education*, Mar. 7, 2003, https://www.chronicle.com/article/Combatants-Become -Allies/35994.

14. "City of Washington/Washington & Jefferson College Blueprint for Collaboration," Nov. 2002. This report was supported by the Claude Worthington Benedum Foundation and developed a shared vision for the community.

15. Richard Florida, *The Rise of the Creative Class: And How It's Transforming Work, Leisure, Community and Everyday Life* (New York: Basic Books, 2002).

16. Brian C. Mitchell, "Colleges as Good Neighbors: Why Towns Matter," *Huffington Post*, Sept. 30, 2012, https://www.huffpost.com/entry/colleges-as-good -neighbor_b_1721309.

17. Judith Rodin, former president of Penn, led a successful and highly admired campaign to integrate the West Philadelphia community into the university community and revitalize the neighborhood (Judith Rodin, *The University and Urban Revival: Out of the Ivory Tower and into the Streets* (Philadelphia: University of Pennsylvania Press, 2007)). Another example from Philadelphia is Drexel's role in the development of Schuylkill Yards, a hub for technology and life-sciences companies (Jon Hurdle, "Philadelphia's First Step to a Platform of Innovation," *New York Times*, Feb. 20, 2018, https://www.nytimes.com/2018/02/20/business /philadelphia-commercial-real-estate.html).

18. Mitchell, "Colleges as Good Neighbors: Why Towns Matter." Annual college guidebooks often include student perceptions of their college environment, which include similar types of quotes that can negatively affect perceptions of an institution.

19. A 2018 survey of one hundred US universities found that 90 percent of the surveyed institutions offer courses dedicated to community-engaged teaching and student learning. These courses provide students with expanded opportunities to interact with local community organizations and leaders, making the local community a "classroom" (Joshua J. Yates and Michaela Accardi, *Field Guide for Urban University-Community Partnerships* (Charlottesville, VA, 2019), https://iasculture .org/research/publications/thriving-cities-field-guide).

20. From Thomas Jefferson to Littleton W. Tazewell, Jan. 5, 1805, *Founders Online*, National Archives, accessed Apr. 11, 2019, https://founders.archives.gov /documents/Jefferson/99-01-02-0958; From Thomas Jefferson to Charles Wilson Peale, Jan. 16, 1802, *Founders Online*, National Archives, accessed Oct. 16, 2019, https://founders.archives.gov/?q=%E2%80%9Cthe%20most%20extensive%20 and%20liberal%20scale%E2%80%9D%20&s=2511311211&sa=&r=1&sr=Peale; Thomas Jefferson to Joseph Priestley, Jan. 18, 1800, *Founders Online*, National Archives, accessed Oct. 16, 2019, https://founders.archives.gov/?q=Priestly%20 Recipient%3A%22Priestley%2C%20Joseph%22&s=2511311211&r=7.

21. Act is 7 U.S.C. 321 et seq, https://www.law.cornell.edu/uscode/text/7/304.

22. In most states, both public and private colleges have set up president-based associations at the state level to lobby at state and federal levels. The National Association of Independent Colleges and Universities focuses, for example, on student aid, regulation, and tax policy affecting its members.

23. "Two Decades of Change in Federal and State Higher Education Funding: Recent Trends across Levels of Government," *Pew Charitable Trusts*, Oct. 15, 2019, https://www.pewtrusts.org/en/research-and-analysis/issue-briefs/2019/10/two -decades-of-change-in-federal-and-state-higher-education-funding. For the 2018/19 academic year, for example, the office of Federal Student Aid disbursed over $61 billion dollars in aid to students in public universities through loans, grants, and work-study programs (Federal Student Aid, Title IV Program Volume Reports, https://studentaid.ed.gov/sa/about/data-center/student/title-iv).

24. Brian C. Mitchell, "A Capital Idea: Blending Strategy and Opportunity to Manage College Assets," *College Planning and Management*, Sept. 1, 2013, https:// webcpm.com/articles/2013/09/01/blending-strategy-and-opportunity-to-manage -college-assets.aspx.

25. Ben Gose, "One-Stop Shopping for Campus Housing," *Chronicle of Higher Education*, Jan. 28, 2005, https://www.chronicle.com/article/One-Stop-Shopping -for-Campus/21039; Brian C. Mitchell, "Colleges and the Hotel Business," *World.edu* (blog), Sept. 24, 2013, https://world.edu/colleges-and-the-hotel-business.

26. This can be a complex and sometimes vexing issue. For many senior college officials, how auditors and rating agencies characterize this third-party public -private partnership may negatively impact the college's bond capacity and audit statements. Language, perception, and intent are critical in designing these part- nerships. An institution must get sound advice, especially legal and accounting advice, before entering into a third-party arrangement if these considerations are of great concern.

27. Mitchell, "A Capital Idea: Blending Strategy and Opportunity to Manage College Assets."

28. Apryl Motley, "The Download on Upkeep," *Business Officer*, Dec. 2015, https://businessofficermagazine.org/features/the-download-on-upkeep; Ellen Kollie," Getting Creative with Facilities Financing," *College Planning and Manage- ment*, Oct.1, 2017, https://webcpm.com/articles/2017/10/01/facilities-financing.aspx.

29. Charles G. Renner, "A Few Lessons about Public-Private Partnerships," *Inside Higher Ed*, Jan. 28, 2019, https://www.insidehighered.com/views/2019/01 /28/advice-institutions-embarking-public-private-partnerships-opinion Brian C. Mitchell, "Using Private Investors to Meet Higher Education's Facilities Needs," *Huffington Post*, Apr. 26, 2017, https://www.huffpost.com/entry/using-private -investors-t_b_9771106.

30. If they do begin investing in community-based housing, colleges and uni- versities often face fierce resistance in some localities. In Boston, for example, the

British firm Scape, looking to find an innovative solution to build more third-party residence complexes, is one example (Tom Acitelli, "Independent Dorm Developer in Boston Pivots to Market-Rate Housing," *Curbed Boston*, Oct. 7, 2019, https:// boston.curbed.com/boston-development/2019/10/7/20903226/dorm-developer -scape-boston-apartments).

31. Mary Beth Faller, "Innovative Novus Project Enters Its Next Stage of Development," *ASU Now*, Apr. 23, 2019, https://asunow.asu.edu/20190423-arizona-impact -asu-novus-innovation-corridor-hyatt-groundbreaking. See also Scott Carlson, "Public-Private Partnerships Take New Shapes," *Chronicle of Higher Education*, May 5, 2019, https://www.chronicle.com/article/Public-Private-Partnerships/246240.

32. Lee Gardner, "Small Colleges Risk a Turn to Private Capital to Build Housing," *Chronicle of Higher Education*, Feb. 25, 2016, https://www.chronicle.com /article/Small-Colleges-Risk-a-Turn-to/235465.

33. Ibid.

34. Peter Applebome, "Not Just Another Dorm," *New York Times*, Dec. 24, 2008, https://www.nytimes.com/2009/01/04/education/edlife/cribs-t.html; Lawrence Biemiller, "More Community Colleges Build Residence Halls," *Chronicle of Higher Education*, Apr. 24, 2009, https://www.chronicle.com/article/More-Community -Colleges-Build/36049; Felicia Mello, "Should Community Colleges in California Start Building Student Housing?" KQED News, June 12, 2019, https://www.kqed .org/news/11753881/should-community-colleges-in-california-start-building -student-housing.

35. In the last five years, the debt at public institutions rose by 18 percent, to $145 billion, while debt at private institutions increased by 3 percent, to $95 billion (Jon Marcus, "Why Colleges Are Borrowing Billions," *The Atlantic*, Oct. 10, 2017, https://www.theatlantic.com/education/archive/2017/10/why-colleges-are-borrowing -billions/542352).

36. The USDA Rural Development program provides affordable funding to develop essential community facilities in rural areas. Funds can be used to purchase, construct, and/or improve essential community facilities, such as museums, libraries or private schools. See "Community Facilities Direct Loan and Grant Program," USDA (website), https://www.rd.usda.gov/programs-services/community -facilities-direct-loan-grant-program

37. In 2008, Massachusetts governor Deval Patrick made a ten-year, $1 billion public funding commitment to develop the Massachusetts Life Sciences Center, which was continued by his successor, Charlie Baker (Max Stendahl, "Gov. Baker Signs $500M, 5-Year Life Sciences Bill," *Boston Business Journal*, June 15, 2018, https://www.bizjournals.com/boston/news/2018/06/15/gov-baker-signs-500m-5 -year-life-sciences-bill.html.

38. Sohvi Heaton, Donald S. Siegel, and David J. Teece, "Universities and Innovation Ecosystems: A Dynamic Capabilities Perspective," *Industrial and Corporate Change* 28, no. 4 (2019): 921–39.

39. Cindy George, "How Rice University Tethered Houston to Space," TMC News, June 28, 2019, https://www.tmc.edu/news/2019/06/how-rice-university -tethered-houston-to-space.

40. Christopher M. Cirillo, "Birth of an Idea: The Creation of Research Triangle Park and Its Sustained Economic Impact on the Research Triangle Area," *Urban Economics*, Apr. 28, 2013, https://sites.duke.edu/urbaneconomics/?p=899; "North Carolina's Research Triangle Park," in *Best Practice in State and Regional Innovation Initiatives: Competing in the 21st Century*, ed. Charles W. Wessner (Washington, DC: National Academies Press, 2013), 231–40.

41. The concept for the academy as an institution of higher education originated in Plato's school of philosophy, founded in the fourth century BCE near Athens, Greece (Lewis Trelawny-Cassity, "Plato: The Academy," *The Internet Encyclopedia of Philosophy*, https://www.iep.utm.edu/academy).

Chapter 6. Accreditors, Athletic Conferences, and Beyond

1. US Department of Education, "Table 303.90. Fall enrollment and number of degree-granting postsecondary institutions, by control and religious affiliation of institution: Selected years, 1980 through 2017," in National Center for Education Statistics, *Digest of Education Statistics* (2018 ed.), https:// nces.ed.gov/programs /digest/d18/tables/dt18_303.90.asp.

2. Council for Higher Education Accreditation, "Regional Accrediting Organi- zations," https://www.chea.org/regional-accrediting-organizations-accreditor-type.

3. Frank C. Abbott, *A History of the Western Interstate Commission for Higher Education: The First Forty Years* (Boulder, CO.: WICHE, 2004), 1.

4. Ibid.

5. Southern Association of Colleges and Schools Commission on Colleges, "The Principles of Accreditation: Foundations for Quality Enhancement," Dec. 2017, https://sacscoc.org/app/uploads/2019/08/2018PrinciplesOfAcreditation.pdf

6. Higher Learning Commission, "Choosing a Pathway for Reaffirmation of Accreditation," https://www.hlcommission.org/Accreditation/choosing-a-pathway .html

7. Higher Learning Commission, "AQIP Pathway Overview," https://www .hlcommission.org/Accreditation/aqip-overview.html.

8. American Bar Association, "The Law School Accreditation Process," Amer- ican Bar Association Section of Legal Education and Admissions to the Bar, Sept. 2016, https://www.americanbar.org/content/dam/aba/publications/misc/legal _education/2016_accreditation_brochure_final.authcheckdam.pdf.

9. David Glenn, "Discipline by Discipline, Accreditors Multiply," *Chronicle of Higher Education*, July 24, 2011, https://www.chronicle.com/article/As-Accreditors -in-Particular/128377.

10. William H. Honan, "Some Say College Accreditation Is Out of Control," *New York Times*, Nov. 11, 1998, https://www.nytimes.com/1998/11/11/us/some-say-college -accreditation-is-out-of-control.html?searchResultPosition=1

11. Ibid.

12. Higher Learning Commission, "Financial and Non-financial Indicators," https://www.hlcommission.org/Accreditation/indicators.html.

13. Middle States Commission on Higher Education, "MSCHE Response to COVID-19 (CORONAVIRUS)," https://www.msche.org/covid-19/.

14. The National Collegiate Athletic Association, "What Is the NCAA?," NCAA (website), http://www.ncaa.org/about/resources/media-center/ncaa-101/what-ncaa; National Association of Intercollegiate Athletics, "2020–21 NAIA Member Institutions," July 14, 2020, https://www.naia.org/schools/files/2020-21_NAIA_Member _Institutions.pdf.

15. Michael Whitmer, "Harvard and Yale Crews Celebrate the 150th Boat Race," *Boston Globe*, June 6, 2015, https://www.bostonglobe.com/sports/2015/06/06 /harvard-and-yale-crews-celebrate-boat-race/uFRfgEVkENrWKXAUDoQVPK /story.html.

16. The National Collegiate Athletic Association, "NCAA Division I," NCAA (website), http://www.ncaa.org/about?division=d1.

17. The National Collegiate Athletic Association, "About NCAA Division II," NCAA (website), http://www.ncaa.org/about?division=d2.

18. The National Collegiate Athletic Association, "About Division III," NCAA (website), http://www.ncaa.org/about?division=d3.

19. Brian Burnsed, "Athletics Departments That Make More Than They Spend Still a Minority," NCAA (website), Sept. 18, 2015, http://www.ncaa.org/about /resources/media-center/news/athletics-departments-make-more-they-spend -still-minority.

20. Ibid.

21. Will Hobson, "Fund and Games," *Washington Post*, Mar. 19, 2015, https:// www.washingtonpost.com/graphics/sports/ncaa-money.

22. The National Collegiate Athletic Association, "NCAA Demographics Database," NCAA (website), Mar. 2020, http://www.ncaa.org/about/resources/research /ncaa-demographics-database.

23. Hobson, "Fund and Games."

24. Ibid.

25. Taylor Branch, "The Shame of College," *The Atlantic*, Oct. 2011, https:// www.theatlantic.com/magazine/archive/2011/10/the-shame-of-college-sports /308643/.

26. Jemele Hill, "The NCAA Had to Cut Athletes a Better Deal," *The Atlantic*, Oct. 30, 2019, https://www.theatlantic.com/ideas/archive/2019/10/ncaa-had-cut -student-athletes-better-deal/601036/.

27. Ibid.

28. Alan Blinder, "How College Sports Spurred Mississippi to Seriously Reconsider Its Flag," *New York Times*, June 27, 2020, https://www.nytimes.com/2020/06 /27/sports/ncaafootball/mississippi-flag-ncaa.html.

29. Rick Rojas, "Mississippi Governor Signs Law to Remove Flag with Confeder-

ate Emblem," *New York Times*, July 15, 2020, https://www.nytimes.com/2020/06/30/us/mississippi-flag.html.

30. Association of American Colleges and Universities, *2018–22 Strategic Plan* (Washington, DC, 2018), https://www.aacu.org/sites/default/files/files/about/AACU_StrategicPlan_2018-22.pdf.

31. Ibid.

32. "Government Relations" Council of Independent Colleges in Virginia, accessed Aug. 3, 2020, http://www.cicv.org/Government-Relations.aspx.

33. "Legislative Agenda," Independent Colleges and Universities of Texas, accessed Aug. 3, 2020, https://www.icut.org/about-icut/legislative-agenda/.

34. "AICUP Member Preferred (AMP)," Association of Independent Colleges and Universities of Pennsylvania, accessed Aug. 3, 2020, http://www.aicup.org/Collaboration/AICUP-Member-Preferred.

35. "The Covenant between Lyon College and the Synod of the Sun, Presbyterian Church," accessed Aug. 3, 2020, https://assets.speakcdn.com/assets/2433/covenant.pdf.

36. Elizabeth Redden, "SMU Sued for Severing Ties with Church," *Inside Higher Ed*, Dec. 9, 2019, https://www.insidehighered.com/news/2019/12/09/smu-sued-amending-governance-documents-separate-itself-church-authority.

37. South Central Jurisdictional Conference of the United Methodist Church v. Southern Methodist University, DC-19-19359 (2019), https://www.insidehighered.com/sites/default/server_files/media/smu_lawsuit.pdf.

38. Ibid.

39. Ibid.

40. Andy Thomason, "Is College President 'the Toughest Job in the Nation?'" *Chronicle of Higher Education*, May 1, 2018, https://www.chronicle.com/article/Is-College-President-the/243289.

41. "2019 ALCF Annual Conference," Wittenberg University, accessed Aug. 3, 2020, https://www.wittenberg.edu/alcf.

Chapter 7. Measuring Success

1. Maltz Auctions, *Former Campus of Green Mountain College* (Central Islip, NY, 2020).

2. Jeffrey K. Liker, *The Toyota Way* (New York: McGraw-Hill Education, 2004), xv.

3. Robert Zemsky, Susan Shaman, and Susan Campbell Baldridge, *The College Stress Test* (Baltimore: Johns Hopkins University Press, 2020), 2.

4. Ibid., 24.

5. Carter Coudriet and Matt Schifrin, "Forbes' 2019 College Financial Health Grades: How Fit Is Your School?," *Forbes*, Nov. 27, 2019, https://www.forbes.com/sites/cartercoudriet/2019/11/27/how-fit-is-your-school-the-methodology-behind-forbes-2019-college-financial-health-grades/#32b0732d61c4.

6. Ibid.

7. Carter Coudriet and Matt Schifrin, "Dawn of the Dead: For Hundreds of the

Nation's Private Colleges, It's Merge or Perish," *Forbes*, Nov. 27, 2019, https://www
.forbes.com/sites/schifrin/2019/11/27/dawn-of-the-dead-for-hundreds-of-the
-nations-private-colleges-its-merge-or-perish/#459160f4770d.

8. Zemsky, Shaman, and Baldridge, *The College Stress Test*, 12.

9. Allen Schick, "A Surplus, If We Can Keep It: How the Federal Budget Surplus Happened," Brookings Institution, Dec. 1, 2000, https://www.brookings.edu
/articles/a-surplus-if-we-can-keep-it-how-the-federal-budget-surplus-happened/.

10. National Center for Educational Statistics, "Undergraduate Enrollment,"
NCES, May 2020, https://nces.ed.gov/programs/coe/indicator_cha.asp.

11. John Hanc, "For Some Colleges, the Best Move Is to Merge," *New York Times*,
Oct. 10, 2019, https://www.nytimes.com/2019/10/10/education/learning/colleges
-mergers.html

12. Staci Provezis, "Augustana College: An Assessment Review Committee's
Role in Engaging Faculty," National Institute for Learning Outcomes Assessment,
July 2011, https://www.learningoutcomesassessment.org/wp-content/uploads/2019
/08/AugustanaCollegeCaseStudy.pdf.

13. Ibid., 3.

14. Dawn Geronimo Terkla, "What Performance Indicators Do Institutions and
Their Boards Commonly Use?" *Trusteeship*, Jan.–Feb. 2011, p. 12, https://agb.org
/trusteeship-article/making-metrics-matter-how-to-use-indicators-to-govern
-effectively/.

15. "Jacobellis v. Ohio," Wikipedia, accessed Aug. 6, 2020, https://en.wikipedia
.org/wiki/Jacobellis_v._Ohio.

Chapter 8. Innovation

1. A 2019 study conducted by the Council for Higher Education Accreditation
describes how accreditors currently review a variety of offerings related to innovation, including distance education, competency-based education, direct assessment with prior learning, and programs that rely heavily on virtual or augmented
environments ("Innovation in Accreditation and Higher Education: Accrediting
Organizations Describe Their Engagement," 2019, https://docs.google.com/gview
?embedded=true&url=https://www.chea.org/sites/default/files/pdf/Innovation-in
-Accreditation-and-Higher-Education_7.10.2019_0.pdf). Michael Horn and Alana
Dunagan use a number of case studies to argue how accreditation can stifle innovation ("Innovation and Quality Assurance in Higher Education," June 2018 https://
www.christenseninstitute.org/wp-content/uploads/2018/06/accreditation_alana
_final_final.pdf).

2. According to a 2019 *Inside Higher Ed* article, for example, more than two hundred institutions have chief innovation officers, and as many colleges have senior
roles related to online learning and academic innovation (Allison Dulin Salisbury
and Terah Crews, "How Higher Ed Can Change Faster," *Inside Higher Ed*, Feb. 27,
2019, https://www.insidehighered.com/digital-learning/views/2019/02/27/how
-colleges-can-use-innovation-labs-drive-change-opinion).

3. A 2018 report by the Council of Independent Colleges provides numerous examples of colleges that have adapted, categorizing key innovations in eight areas: athletics, career connections, community engagement, consortia arrangement, cost containment, curricular reform, new academic program, new student populations (Barbara Hetrick, Philip M. Katz, and S. Georgia Nugent, *Innovation and the Independent College: Examples from the Sector* (Washington, DC: CIC, 2018)).

4. Recent discussions concerning the perception that institutions of higher education are notoriously slow to change include Steven Mintz, "Why Innovations Fail: Ten Hard-Won Lessons," *Chronicle of Higher Education*, July 23, 2019, https://www.insidehighered.com/blogs/higher-ed-gamma/why-innovations-fail; William G. Bowen and Eugene M. Tobin, *Locus of Authority: The Evolution of Faculty Roles in the Governance of Higher Education* (Princeton, NJ: Princeton University Press, 2015); David Schejbal, "Challenges to Change and Innovation in Higher Education," *EvoLLLution*, Feb. 8, 2013, https://evolllution.com/opinions/challenges-change-innovation-higher-education.

5. Michael M. Crow and William B. Dabars, *Designing the New American University* (Baltimore: John Hopkins University Press, 2015).

6. Clayton Christensen and Henry J. Eyring, *The Innovative University: Changing the DNA of Higher Education* (San Francisco: Jossey-Bass, 2011).

7. Richard A. DeMillo, *Revolution in Higher Education: How A Small Band of Innovators Will Make College Accessible and Affordable* (Cambridge, MA: MIT Press, 2015), 11. The *New York Times* also acknowledged the importance of 2012 for MOOCs (Laura Pappano, "The Year of the MOOC," *New York Times*, Nov. 4, 2012, https://www.nytimes.com/2012/11/04/education/edlife/massive-open-online-courses-are-multiplying-at-a-rapid-pace.html).

8. David J. Staley, *Alternative Universities: Speculative Design for Innovation in Higher Education* (Baltimore: Johns Hopkins University Press, 2019).

9. Ibid., 12.

10. Cathy Davidson, *The New Education: How to Revolutionize the University to Prepare Students for a World in Flux* (New York: Basic Books, 2017); Stephen M. Gavazzi and E. Gordon Gee, *Land-Grant Universities for the Future* (Baltimore: Johns Hopkins University Press, 2018).

11. Colleen Flaherty, "The New, New Education," *Inside Higher Ed*, Aug. 24, 2017, https://www.insidehighered.com/news/2017/08/24/cathy-davidson%E2%80%99s-new-book-manifesto-teaching-students-and-institutions-how-survive.

12. Zack Friedman, "Student Loan Debt Statistics in 2020: A Record $1.6 Trillion," *Forbes*, Feb. 3, 2020, https://www.forbes.com/sites/zackfriedman/2020/02/03/student-loan-debt-statistics/#8250627281fe.

13. Scott Carlson, "What Higher Ed Can Learn from Health Care," *Chronicle of Higher Education*, Feb. 2, 2020, https://www.chronicle.com/article/What-Higher-Ed-Can-Learn-From/247951; Kellie Woodhouse, "Health Care and Higher Ed: The Two Industries Differ in Key Ways but Face Several Similar and Pressing Challenges,"

Inside Higher Ed, July 20, 2015, https://www.insidehighered.com/news/2015/07/20
/health-care-and-higher-education-face-similar-challenges-and-transformations.

14. CASE is a global nonprofit association composed of educational institutions that serves professionals in the field of advancement. It offers a variety of services to its members, including conferences and training materials.

15. How boards make these recommendations is critical. Boards must maintain a healthy tension between themselves and their university's president in order to set policy without micromanaging. One way is to suggest that policy changes be linked to an emerging strategic plan.

16. Recent notable examples of major donors that have funded innovative programs include George Soros's $1-billion donation to the Open Society University Network (Elizabeth Redden, "Open Society University Network Launched with $1 Billion Gift," *Inside Higher Ed*, Feb. 4, 2020, https://www.insidehighered.com /news/2020/02/04/amid-authoritarian-resurgence-george-soros-pledges-1-billion -toward-new-university), and Stewart and Lynda Resnick's $750-million pledge to Caltech to support research in the area of environmental sustainability (Kathy Svitil, "Stewart and Lynda Resnick Pledge $750 Million to Caltech to Support Environmental Sustainability Research," *Caltech Matters*, Sept. 26, 2019, https:// www.caltech.edu/about/news/stewart-and-lynda-resnick-pledge-750-million -caltech-support-environmental-sustainability-research).

17. Kellie Woodhouse, "New Push for Trustee Training," *Inside Higher Ed*, July 7, 2015, https://www.insidehighered.com/news/2015/07/07/states-explore-required -training-university-board-members; Marjorie Valbrun, "Does USC Need More Housecleaning?," *Inside Higher Ed*, May 21, 2019, https://www.insidehighered.com /news/2019/05/21/usc-board-trustees-undergo-major-changes-wake-recent -scandals.

18. In addition to the works by Christensen and Eyring, Crow and Dabars, DeMillo, and Staley cited above, see Matthew Wisnioski and Lee Vinsel, "The Campus Innovation Myth," *Chronicle of Higher Education*, June 11, 2019, https:// www-chronicle-com.ezproxy.library.wisc.edu/interactives/20190611-vinsel; Paul Basken, "Harvard's Allston Expansion 'the next great innovation centre,'" *Times Higher Education*, Oct. 28, 2018, https://www.timeshighereducation.com/harvards -allston-expansion-next-great-innovation-centre.

19. Massive Open Online Courses (MOOCs) are, as their name suggests, classes delivered online open to unlimited participants. Education entrepreneurs like Richard DeMillo touted MOCCs as radically disruptive technology (*Revolution in Higher Education*), but their success and impact to date has been much less significant than advocates predicted.

20. Dan Zaiontz, *#FollowTheLeader: Lessons in Social Media Success from #HigherEd CEOs* (Saint Louis, MO: EDUniverse Media, 2015).

21. James Paterson, "Tuition Discounts Reach Record High (Again) as Colleges Diversify Revenue," *EducationDive*, May 10, 2019, https://www.educationdive.com

/news/tuition-discounts-reach-record-high-again-as-colleges-diversify-revenue
/554523/; Scott Jaschik, "2019 Survey of Admissions Leaders: The Pressure Grows,"
Inside Higher Ed, Sep. 23, 2019, https://www.insidehighered.com/news/survey/2019
-survey-admissions-leaders-pressure-grows; Zack Friedman, "Student Loan Debt
Statistics in 2020: A Record $1.6 Trillion," *Forbes*, Feb. 3, 2020, https://www.forbes
.com/sites/zackfriedman/2020/02/03/student-loan-debt-statistics/#20573e89281f.

Chapter 9. Why Leadership Matters

1. Notable coverage on initial reactions to the pandemic in higher education include Lee Gardner, "Inside the Scramble for Students," *Chronicle of Higher Education*, May 18, 2020, https://www.chronicle.com/article/Inside-the-Scramble-for /248801; Paul N. Friga, "Under Covid-19, University Budgets Like We've Never Seen Before," *Chronicle of Higher Education*, Apr. 20, 2020, https://www-chronicle-com .ezproxy.library.wisc.edu/article/Under-Covid-19-University/248574; Emma Whitford, "Here Come the Furloughs," *Inside Higher Ed*, Apr. 10, 2020, https://www .insidehighered.com/news/2020/04/10/colleges-announce-furloughs-and-layoffs -financial-challenges-mount.

2. At least two small colleges permanently closed at the end of the spring 2020 semester, and many more were in peril (Emma Whitford, "How Much Did Coronavirus Disruptions Affect 2 Closing Colleges?," *Inside Higher Ed*, Apr. 2, 2020, https:// www.insidehighered.com/news/2020/04/02/two-small-colleges-winding-down -operations-coronavirus-impact-looms-over-higher-ed; Deirdre Fernandes, "Amid Coronavirus Pandemic, a Growing List of Colleges in Financial Peril," *Boston Globe*, May 8, 2020, https://www.bostonglobe.com/2020/05/08/metro/amid-pandemic -growing-list-colleges-financial-peril). See also Robert Kelchen, "This Will Be One of the Worst Months in the History of Higher Education," *Chronicle of Higher Education*, July 7, 2020, https://www.chronicle.com/article/this-will-be-one-of-the -worst-months-in-the-history-of-higher-education; Amy Whyte, "Universities Were 'Not Prepared' for This Crisis," *Institutional Investor*, Mar. 27, 2020, https://www .institutionalinvestor.com/article/b1kybhrtgmnzc8/Universities-Were-Not-Prepared -for-This-Crisis

3. Brian C. Mitchell, "The Responsibility of Choosing a College President in Times of Crisis," *Trusteeship* 24, no. 4 (2020): 42, 47.

4. In addition to the general resources for boards, the Association of Governing Boards created substantial resources on navigating the COVID-19 crisis: https://agb .org/knowledge-center/trending-topics/coronavirus-resources-for-higher-education -boards/.

5. Billy Witz and Gillian R. Brassil, "Stanford Permanently Cuts 11 Sports amid Coronavirus Pandemic," *New York Times*, July 8, 2020, https://www.nytimes .com/2020/07/08/sports/coronavirus-stanford-cuts.html.

6. Colleges and universities are the largest employers in ten states and in two-thirds of America's one-hundred largest cities, see: AGB, "Higher Education Contributes to a Strong Economy," Guardians Campaign, June 6, 2019, https://agb

.org/guardians-campaign/higher-education-contributes-to-a-strong-economy
/#:~:text=Here's%20how%3A%20About%20one%20million,dining%2C%20retail
%2C%20and%20transportation.

7. A 2018 study found that the University of California system, Johns Hopkins institutions, the University of Michigan, and the University of Wisconsin, for example, were the largest employers in their respective states (Casey Leins, "These Are the Largest Employers in Every State," *USNews*, Dec. 21, 2018, https://www .usnews.com/news/best-states/articles/2018-12-21/walmart-health-companies-and -universities-are-top-state-employers-study-finds).

8. Two examples of how American political polarization extended to higher education in 2020 include suggestions to examine the tax-exempt status of non-profit colleges and universities, and the rescinded directive to require international students to transfer or leave the US if their schools held classes entirely online because of the COVID-19 pandemic; Paul Fain, "Trump Threatens Tax Exemption of Colleges," *Inside Higher Ed*, July 13, 2020, https://www.insidehighered.com /quicktakes/2020/07/13/trump-threatens-tax-exemption-colleges; Collin Binkley, "Trump Administration Rescinds Rule on Foreign Students," AP News, July 14, 2020, https://apnews.com/38b6562b7aaa73ea66fb72b06472e05d.

9. Francie Diep, "How Higher Ed Can Fight Racism: 'Speak Up When It's Hard'" *Chronicle of Higher Education*, June 30, 2020, https://www.chronicle.com/article /How-Higher-Ed-Can-Fight/248897; Marcia A. Wilson and Lurraine Jones, "Dear Senior University Leaders: What Will You Say You Did to Address Racism in Higher Education?," *THE*, June 9, 2020, https://www.timeshighereducation.com/write -times-higher-education.

10. Rick Seltzer, "Mass. Governor Signs College Closure Law," *Inside Higher Ed*, Nov. 18, 2019, https://hechingerreport.org/black-college-presidents-matter-we -should-lead-from-the-top/.

11. The Higher Learning Commission shifted its financial indicator process in response the COVID-19 pandemic (https://www.hlcommission.org/Accreditation /indicators.html); Paul Fain and Doug Lederman, "Suspension of Financial Responsibility Scores?" *Inside Higher Ed*, Apr. 2, 2020, https://www.insidehighered.com /news/2020/04/02/college-groups-push-suspension-financial-responsibility-scores -feds-release-distance.

12. By summer 2020, the Ivy League cancelled fall sports (Greta Anderson, "Ivy League Postpones Athletics until 2021," *Inside Higher Ed*, July 9, 2020; https://www .insidehighered.com/news/2020/07/09/ivy-league-will-not-play-fall-sports-2020).

13. As noted in our first book, tuition increasingly subsidizes athletics, and only one in eight of the 202 Division I colleges took in more revenue than was spent on athletics between the years 2005 and 2010 (Brian C. Mitchell and W. Joseph. King, *How to Run a College: A Practical Guide for Trustees, Faculty, Administrators, and Policymakers* [Baltimore: Johns Hopkins University Press, 2018], 109).

14. Emily Bazelon, "What Will College Be like in the Fall?," *New York Times Magazine*, June 25, 2020, https://www.nytimes.com/2020/06/03/magazine/covid

-college-fall.html; José Antonio Bowen, "5 Bigger and Better Ideas for Fall 2020," *Inside Higher Ed*, July 20, 2020, https://www.insidehighered.com/views/2020/07/20 /college-leaders-should-consider-some-outside-box-ideas-fall-2020-opinion; David Rosowsky, "Countdown to Fall 2020: Higher Ed Gambles on Its Future," *Forbes*, July 7, 2020, https://www.forbes.com/sites/davidrosowsky/2020/07/07/countdown -to-fall-2020-higher-ed-gambles-on-its-future/#5fd54db0319f.

Page numbers in *italics* refer to figures.

change agent president: duties of, 13–14; qualities of, 11, 13, 13, 14; strategic planning and, 28, 55

chief business officer (CBO), 46–47

chief financial officer (CFO): president and, 21, 63; provosts and, 68–69; responsibilities of, 21, 47–48, 65, 135, 136; survey of, 96, 158n10

chief innovation officers, 183n2

Cho, Fujio, 110

Christensen, Clayton, 126

church-related peer institutions, 106

Clausewitz, Carl von, 29

code of ethics, 43–44

colleges and universities: as academic enterprise, 21–22; adaptability of, 133; administration of, 10; assessment of, 108, 112–14, 141, 178n26; vs. businesses, 142; community engagement, 75, 76–77, 78, 79–80, 142, 177n19; COVID-19 pandemic and, ix, 141–42, 148, 186n2; crisis management, 65–66; cultural and social impact of, 65, 153, 154; demographic trends and, 3; economic impact of, 186n6, 187n7; financial management of, xi, 1, 42, 57, 71, 88, 151, 157n7; funding of, 83, 84–85; future direction of, 116, 149; innovative culture, 132–33; institutional sustainability, 149–50; intellectual capital, 150; mergers and acquisitions, 118–19; mission of, 83; performance indicators dashboards, 121; policy formulation, 142–43; public image of, 77, 83; public-private partnerships, 87–89, 178n30; racial and ethnic segregation, x, 102; regulation of, 150–51; religious affiliations, 92–93, 104–6; reorganization of, 54–55; research facilities, 77; response to failure of, 116–18; strategic vision, 55, 83; structure of, 51; tax-exempt status of, 81, 82, 85

college sports: athletic associations and conferences, 92, 96–98, 100, 101; coaches, 99, 100; cost and benefits of, 97, 98–100, 187n13; facilities, 99; inequity in, 100; popularity of, 97; presidents and, 98–99; racial tensions and, 101; role in society, 99–100, 151; tension between academics and, 23

College Stress Test, 111–12

collegiality tradition, 51–52, 56

Columbia University, 52

community colleges, 89, 130

community relations: benefits of, 90; board of trustees' approach to, 79–80; challenges of, 77–78; economic impact of, 77–79, 82, 177n17; issue of control, 87–88; leadership and, 80, 90; president's role in, 80, 81; role of circumstances in, 86–87; social and cultural impact of, 80, 81–83, 91; stakeholders of, 78, 90–91; strategic planning and, 19, 87; time commitment to, 90; town/gown tensions, 19, 89, 175n3; town/gown tensions in, 19, 89, 175n3

Consumer Price Index (CPI), 109

convenience institutions, 111–12

Cooper, Preston, 3

Council for Advancement and Support of Education (CASE), 46, 129, 172n13, 185n14

Council for Aid to Education, 45–46

Council for Higher Education Accreditation, 93

Council of Independent Colleges, xv, 70, 184n3

Council of Independent Colleges in Virginia (CICV), 103

COVID-19 pandemic: economic impact of, 42, 96, 142; higher education and, ix, 49, 65, 85, 186n2; online resources, 186n4; social impact of, xi, 141

Coyne, Kevin, 114

creative thinking, 33

Crow, Michael: *Designing the New American University*, 126

Culverhouse, Hugh F., Jr., 172n12

Dabars, William, 126

Davidson, Cathy, 127

De Bono, Edward, 33

Degree Analytics, 47

DeMillo, Richard, 126–27, 185n19

Deval Patrick, 179n37

Dewey, John, 7

Disney, 33, 126

Diversity Innovation Grants, 40

donors, 19–20, 45, 46, 66, 74–75, 172n12, 185n16